THEODORE
ROETHKE'S
FAR FIELDS

THEODORE

ROETHKE'S

FAR FIELDS

The Evolution of His Poetry

PETER BALAKIAN

LOUISIANA STATE UNIVERSITY PRESS
Baton Rouge and London

First printing

98 97 96 95 94 93 92 91 90 89   5 4 3 2 1

Designer: Laura Roubique Gleason
Typeface: Palatino
Typesetter: The Composing Room of Michigan, Inc.
Printer: Thomson-Shore, Inc.
Binder: John H. Dekker & Sons, Inc.

Library of Congress Cataloging-in-Publication Data

Balakian, Peter, 1951–
    Theodore Roethke's far fields: the evolution of his poetry /
Peter Balakian.
        p.   cm.
    Includes index.
    ISBN 0-8071-2454-0 (pbk)
    1. Roethke, Theodore, 1908–1963—Criticism and interpretation.
I. Title.
PS3535.039Z56   1989
811'.52—dc19   88-29212
                                                                           CIP

The paper in this book meets the guidelines for permanence and durability of the
Committee on Production Guidelines for Book Longevity of the Council on Library
Resources.∞

Chapters Six and Two originally appeared as "Theodore Roethke's 'Meditations of an
Old Woman': The Mask and Its Cracks," in CEA Critic, XLVII (Spring, 1985), and
"Theodore Roethke, William Carlos Williams, and the American Grain," in Modern
Language Studies, XVII (Winter, 1987), respectively. Previously unpublished material
by William Carlos Williams, copyright © 1988 by William Eric Williams and Paul H.
Williams, used by permission of New Directions Pub. Corp., Agents. Excerpts of
poems by William Carlos Williams in Imaginations, copyright © 1970 by Florence H.
Williams, reprinted by permission of New Directions Pub. Corp. Previously pub-
lished material by Theodore Roethke copyright © 1937, 1954, 1957, 1958, 1959, 1960,
1961, 1962, 1963, 1964, 1965, 1966 by Beatrice Roethke as Administratix of the Estate of
Theodore Roethke, copyright © 1932, 1934, 1935, 1936, 1937, 1938, 1939, 1940, 1941,
1942, 1946, 1947, 1948, 1949, 1950, 1951, 1952, 1953, 1954, 1955, 1956, 1957, 1958, 1961
by Theodore Roethke—all reprinted by permission of Doubleday and Faber and
Faber from Collected Poems by Theodore Roethke. Published poems from which ex-
cerpts are taken appeared originally in the following: The American Scholar: "Big
Wind," copyright 1947 by The United Chapters of Phi Beta Kappa. The New Republic:
"Carnations," "Child on Top of a Green House," "Flower-Dump," "Weed Puller,"
"Moss Gathering," copyright 1946 by Editorial Publications, Inc. The Commonweal:
"Double Feature," as "Episode Seven," copyright 1942 by Commonweal Publishing
Co., Inc. The Tiger's Eye: "A Field of Light," copyright 1948 by The Tiger's Eye. Harper's
Bazaar: "My Papa's Waltz," copyright 1942 by Hearst Magazines, Inc. American Mer-
cury: "Pickle Belt," copyright 1943 by The American Mercury, Inc. Partisan Review,
Botteghe Oscure, "The Other," copyright © 1956 by Botteghe Oscure. Excerpts from
Selected Letters of Theodore Roethke, ed. Ralph J. Mills, copyright © 1968 by University of
Washington Press and from On the Poet and His Craft, ed. Ralph J. Mills, copyright ©
1965 by University of Washington Press, reprinted by permission of University of
Washington Press.

To Jack Wheatcroft
and to the memory of
Hyatt Waggoner

Contents

Preface

This book is concerned primarily with Theodore Roethke's develop-
ment as an artist. In focusing on Roethke's poetic evolution I have
found that being what I like to think of as "gymnastically eclectic"
has enabled me to move with the sensibility of his various stages of
growth. Hence, I deal with each of his poetic phases in terms that I
believe best illuminate the major aspects of that period's poetic
achievement. It seems to me that the many thesis-oriented books
about Roethke fail to deal with the very nature of the poet's growth
and evolution—an evolution that is unpredictable yet inevitable.
For the broad and rich significance of Roethke's poetry cannot ade-
quately be contained in a single theory or exclusive mode of
interpretation.[1]

My book proceeds from the assumption that Roethke's whole
body of poetry has an organic shape and that the poems, taken in

---

1. The majority of books about Theodore Roethke's poetry consider his work in
terms of a single thesis. Critics have either found it useful to apply an overarching
concept to his work, or they have mistakenly viewed Roethke's poetry as having a
monolithic quality. Richard Allen Blessing's *Theodore Roethke's Dynamic Vision* (Bloom-
ington, Ind., 1974) approaches the entire body of Roethke's work in light of his idea of
"dynamic perception"; Jenijoy La Belle's *The Echoing Wood of Theodore Roethke* (Prince-
ton, N.J., 1976) is essentially a Bloomian reading of Roethke and of his relationship to
tradition; Jay Parini in *Theodore Roethke: An American Romantic* (Amherst, Mass., 1979)
interprets Roethke in the context of American Romanticism; Lynn Ross-Bryant's
Theodore Roethke: Poetry of the Earth, Poet of the Spirit (Port Washington, N.Y., 1981)
concentrates on how Roethke's "poetry of the earth" is connected to his idea of "the
life of the spirit"; Norman Chaney in *Theodore Roethke: The Poetics of Wonder* (Wash-
ington, D.C., 1981) claims that "Roethke's poetry is systematically based on an at-
titude of wonder"; Neal Bowers in *Theodore Roethke: The Journey from I to Otherwise*
(Columbia, Mo., 1981) reads the entire body of poetry as mysticism in poetry form.

sequence, chart a journey which unfolds as the life does, with vicissitudes and oscillations. Dramatic changes occur in his style, of course, but the continuity in his sensibility remains. The shift from the experimental form of the "lost son" poems to the formal metrics of *Words for the Wind*, or the movement from the formal phase to the long free verse lines of "North American Sequence," or the shift back to the metaphysical style of "Sequence, Sometimes Metaphysical" all reveal continuity and evolution. It is the persistent coexistence of continuity and evolution in Roethke's poetry which demands that the critic pay close attention to the unique structures and concerns of each of his evolving phases. My Introduction, which attempts to place Roethke in literary history, is in no way a thesis for this book but rather a speculation on and an interpretation of Roethke's place in modern poetry and his importance to the poetry of our age.

Acknowledgments

I am most indebted to my two teachers, Hyatt H. Waggoner and Jack Wheatcroft, who at different times in my life and in different ways opened up for me the possibilities of Theodore Roethke's poetry. Their astute comments have been immensely helpful to me throughout the course of my work. I am most grateful to my wife, Helen Kebabian, whose editorial expertise has been invaluable to me at every stage of the making of this book. I would like to express, as well, my appreciation to the following: David H. Hirsch for the encouragement and guidance he gave me when I first began thinking about Roethke; Laura Tanner, who carefully proofread a version of the manuscript; the Colgate University Research Council for generously giving me a grant and a leave of absence during which time I was able to complete my work.

Abbreviations

PC

On the Poet and His Craft: Selected Prose of Theodore Roethke, ed. Ralph J. Mills (Seattle, 1965).

SF

Straw for the Fire: From the Notebooks of Theodore Roethke, 1943–1963, ed. David Wagoner (New York, 1974).

SL

Selected Letters of Theodore Roethke, ed. Ralph J. Mills (Seattle, 1968).

THEODORE
ROETHKE'S
FAR FIELDS

INTRODUCTION

Our First Contemporary

Poets' reputations rise and fall with the currents of aesthetic fashion, the prevailing winds of critical methodology, and the vicissitudes of religious and philosophical world views. Of course reputations are not always an indication of artistic achievement, and the complex cultural processes that canonize writers and cast others into oblivion are not always just or reliable. No artist is immune from the relativism of a historical moment, yet I believe that truly significant art of a previous era will continue to define a part of the present and in doing so will transcend the relativism of any historical moment.

The complex reasons for the present decline in Roethke's reputation as a poet are not my concern here. Yet I find it odd that the judgments of some of our most influential critics of twentieth-century poetry find him to be a poet of lesser importance and do not accord him the value a poetic harbinger deserves. No doubt the current trend toward critical methodologies based on linguistic theory and tied to a tradition of French rationalism has had something to do with a milieu that is not particularly sympathetic to the kind of poetry Roethke has written. His intuitive psychology, lyrical language, and suprarational view of the universe do not seem suitable for critics engaged in the rational methods of linguistic analysis. It may be true, too, that Roethke's shifts in style and idiom—what may appear to be a lack of external harmony within the body of his work—during the five decades in which he wrote have made him difficult for critics to categorize. Although I do not see Roethke through a hagiographer's lens, I do believe his rightful place is that of an innovative poet who has been a major source of influence on the poetry of our time.

One can argue forcefully, as I wish to, that no single book of poems is as important to the evolution of the idioms that have dominated American poetry in the four decades following World War II than is *The Lost Son and Other Poems*, published in 1948. Most of these poems were written and published in American magazines and journals in the early and mid-forties.

Hyatt H. Waggoner and James E. B. Breslin have portrayed accurately the shift in American poetry that became apparent by the mid-fifties and marked an end to the final phase of modernism that was waning by the late forties.[1] Certainly Allen Ginsberg's *Howl* (1956) and Robert Lowell's *Life Studies* (1959) are landmarks in their rejection of the autotelic, symbolistic, and purportedly impersonal poetry of late modernism. Ginsberg and Lowell were concerned with breaking down the barriers between life and art and finding a representative identity that was more subjective and personal than that which T. S. Eliot, Ezra Pound, Robert Frost, William Carlos Williams, or Wallace Stevens had created. By the late fifties and early sixties Ginsberg, Lowell, John Berryman, Sylvia Plath, Anne Sexton, Denise Levertov, James Dickey, James Wright, and Robert Bly, to name several, were proceeding along new lines. They were writing poetry that was more openly autobiographical and personally emotional; their poems reflected a sense that poetic language was part of a life process; their language was more demotic and their diction more colloquial. As Breslin puts it, they sought "ways of ordering poetry that [would] not stifle consciousness" and "new ways of binding form and flux so that temporality will not seem to have been violated."[2]

Not only did the subject of the poet's past become important, but also material of the poet's family became significant to this new poetry. In the way that inherited Western cultural myths, symbols, and history were crucial to the modernist poet's sense of the past, experience derived from personally inherited history—blood history—became central to the postmodern poet's idea of the past. The impact of World War II, the nightmare of the Holocaust, and the

1. See Hyatt H. Waggoner, *American Poets: From Puritanism to the Present* (Baton Rouge, 1984), Chap. XXI, and James E. B. Breslin, *From Modern to Contemporary: American Poetry, 1945–1965* (Chicago, 1984), Chaps. 1–3.
2. Breslin, *From Modern to Contemporary,* 60.

terror created by the atomic and now nuclear age, seem to have discredited for poets much of the meaning and viability accorded Western civilization. For example, the overarching Western myths and texts that stand behind "The Waste Land," "The Cantos," or "The Bridge" became far less meaningful and therefore less usable to American poets after World War II. And if it can be said, as I believe it can, that familial history has supplanted a good deal of cultural history for the poets of our time, then certainly Roethke's *The Lost Son*, Ginsberg's *Kaddish*, and Lowell's *Life Studies* emerge as the seminal family cycles of the era. Each book in its own way is groundbreaking, each uses autobiographical and inherited familial sources to shape a myth out of history, and thus each marks a break with the modernist idea of the past.

Breslin maintains that the evolution of American poetry after modernism can be best understood by dividing the period into five major groups: the beat, confessional, deep image, Black Mountain, and New York schools. In a broad sense, the poetry of these five groups, he argues, characterizes the major poetic reorientation of our period.[3] Although such a paradigm may be too schematic, it gives a perspective on our age and helps make historical sense of Theodore Roethke. If we look at our era in terms of these five movements, which in sum can be said to give definition to the dominant trends, it becomes clear that Roethke in *The Lost Son* had anticipated many of these new directions. (Oddly enough, Breslin fails to discuss Roethke as a significant force in this historical evolution.) For no single book of poems, written at such an early date—a good decade before Lowell and Ginsberg had their breakthroughs—incorporates more of the innovative forms and poetic assumptions that have come to define the contemporary idiom in American poetry.

In *The Lost Son*, Roethke is confessionally Freudian in the manner that would become important to poets like Lowell, Berryman, Plath, Sexton, and Ginsberg. Yet the psychic identity of his persona, the lost son, is based predominantly on Jungian psychology. And it is, of course, the Jungian idea of consciousness that would be embraced by the deep imagists like Bly and Wright and by other

3. *Ibid.*, ix–xv.

poets such as Galway Kinnell, W. S. Merwin, and Charles Simic in their attention to the idea of collective mind. What Roethke described as his "telescopic" method of presentation contains several of the assumptions that lie behind the deep-image technique. And Roethke's protean experiments with form anticipate various elements of the dynamism of open-field form that would become important to the Black Mountain poets.

Roethke's confessional voice in *The Lost Son* grew from the painful experience of his private life. Unlike his modernist predecessors, he did not attempt to transform his personal suffering into a medium that was impersonally mythic or aesthetically self-contained. If emotional trauma and psychic pain are apparent in "Prufrock," "The Broken Tower," or "Sunday Morning," for example, the origins of Eliot's, Crane's, and Stevens' suffering and the private details that would uncover their unique personalities were not their poetic concerns. Conversely, Roethke's poems confront the intimate self and turn the bald sources of experience into grist for the poet's transforming power. Roethke's childhood in his father's greenhouse and his history of mental breakdowns are the central autobiographical events which inform the creation of the lost son.

His father's twenty-five acres of greenhouses in the Saginaw Valley and the hothouse world of peat moss, plant cuttings, carnations, roses, cyclamen, and compost organisms was the loamy place out of which he would shape his mind and delve into his psychic and familial past. The greenhouse became the glass womb in the mind where a lifetime's source of figurative language blossomed into a concept of self. Roethke lived much of his adult life in the throes and cycles of manic depression for which he was periodically hospitalized and on occasion given shock treatment. His battle with life at the mind's edge was a passageway for him into the wilderness of his psyche and soul. With Roethke one is forced to restate an old truth: his mental instability was a source and fuel for his art.

The Freudian kind of confessionalism in *The Lost Son* is realized, to a large degree, in Roethke's ability to make use of traumatic and ecstatic childhood experience and his need to probe his private dream world in order to release psychic tensions and relieve himself of past burdens and repressed guilt. By wrestling with his painful past, he sought a way to confront his father, the greenhouse keeper who haunted his imagination. Although Freudian notions were not unknown to modernists like Eliot and Crane, such a confessional psychology was at most only obliquely associated with the poet's personal life *in the poems*. By contrast Roethke's poetry of confession makes use of the details of autobiography in a way that is significantly different from the modernists.

The psychic life of his persona, the lost son, is defined by the family landscape of Roethke's greenhouse childhood: his father, Otto, whose untimely death left Roethke at age thirteen a lost son; those Old World employees, Max Laurisch, Frau Bauman, Frau Schmidt, and Frau Schwartz, who were horticulturists and extended kin in the poet's memory; and the greenhouse chores—like weed pulling, moss gathering, and transplanting—that as a boy Roethke performed ritualistically and assiduously for his father. The grounding of a poetic cycle in such highly personal concerns would become a common assumption for poets such as Plath, W. D. Snodgrass, Sexton, Lowell, Berryman, and Ginsberg by the late fifties and early sixties. Roethke—like Lowell with his New England Protestant family and Ginsberg and his politically radical Jewish family—is concerned with the mythic shape of his family past and with the archetypal and cultural significance of that past. This psychological and cultural way of transforming family history into confessional poetry also differs significantly from another kind of domestic poetry, often more simple (meditations on wives, husbands, sons, daughters, etc.), that is prevalent in Romantic and Victorian poetry and that has become popular again in the past decade. In short, much of what is innovative about *The Lost Son* stems from Roethke's pioneering this postmodern form of familial confessionalism, which contained at least part of the new era's "new confession," as Emerson once put it. Roethke wrote in a notebook entry:

> I was crazed
> Into meaning more profound than what my fathers heard,
> Those listening bearded men
> Who cut the ground with hoes; and made with hands
> An order out of muck and sand. Those Prussian men
> Who hated uniforms.
> (SF, 50)

This new kind of confessionalism could be successful only if the unveiling of the private life could achieve universality. The naked self and the representative nature of that self must constantly overlap—sometimes fully merged and at other times in a necessarily uneasy tension. It has been well documented that Roethke had, especially during the forties, a deep interest in Jungian psychology, and this interest served his evolving poetics. In creating the lost son, he wished to unite a deeply personal consciousness (a Freudian concept of the mind) with an impersonal or collective idea of the psyche which was based largely on a Jungian concept of the unconscious. This unique merging of Freudian and Jungian psychology in *The Lost Son* anticipates both the Jungian proclivities of Robert Bly's deep imagism and the Freudian confessionalism of Lowell, Ginsberg, Berryman, Plath, and many others.

Numerous times during those years, Roethke recorded his feelings about the nature of the collective mind in the "lost son" poems. He came to believe that one could move forward spiritually only if one returned first to the origins of one's psychic life. He asserted that his new poems oozed out of an "older memory" and "dribbled out of the unconscious" (SL, 130). A world of cosmogonic occurrences and a state of primal feeling defined the evolving personality of the lost son. And his wonderful depiction of his Jungian crow of chaos became a veritable emblem for his art:

> When I saw that clumsy crow
> Flap from a wasted tree,
> A shape in the mind rose up:
> Over the gulfs of dream
> Flew a tremendous bird
> Further and further away
> Into a moonless black,
> Deep in the brain, far back.
> ("Night Crow")

This peculiar blend of Freudian and Jungian concepts evolved out of Roethke's approach to the natural world. Nature became his objective correlative, that medium through which he could forge a confessional voice able to contain a personal self and a representative version of that self—something mythic. Given the realities of

Roethke's childhood, nature would always be a vehicle of the evolving self and a container for the spirit's life and the mind's form.

For Roethke, nature was not only religion brought down to earth, a container of emblematic meanings and an embodiment of human consciousness as it was for Emerson; nature was the script of his life—myth and autobiography bound into one. The natural world was the reality in which his childhood was lived and his family's drama acted out. His Freudian relationship to his parents could not be separated from the stuff in the greenhouse. Because he invented his lost son—the myth of himself—out of the hothouse world his father created, nature became both an emblem of autobiography and the container of a universal soul. He referred to his greenhouse as a "womb, a heaven-on-earth" (PC, 39).

This compelling and idiosyncratic relationship with nature was crucial to his ability to make of the lost son a confessional voice and a mythic mask—a poetic character with what one must term an ontogenetic and a phylogenetic identity. This myth making thus allowed him to turn the lost son into a character with an archetypal heritage whose identity resonates with that large cast of lost sons who have preceded him: Jesus, Job, Oedipus, Telemachus, Hamlet, Huck Finn, Ishmael, Quentin Compson, Stephen Dedalus, to name a few. In seeking his own father and his spiritual Father, the lost son is, in every sense, on a pilgrimage—on a passage at once out of the self and into its mucky interior.

Roethke's ability to create a phylogenetic identity for the lost son and to dramatize a "racial memory" derived to a large degree from his ability to "telescope image and symbol," as he put it. His acute awareness of this technique discloses the degree to which he felt he could penetrate the human psyche and face the mystery in things.

> I believe that, in this kind of poem, the poet, in order to be true to what is most universal in himself, should not rely on allusion; should not comment or employ many judgment words; should not meditate (or maunder). He must scorn being "mysterious" or loosely oracular, but be willing to face up to the genuine mystery. His language must be compelling and immediate: he must create an actuality. He must be able to telescope image and symbol, if necessary, without relying on the obvious connectives: to speak in a kind of psychic shorthand when his pro-

tagonist is under great stress. He must be able to shift his rhythms rapidly, the "tension." (PC, 42)

It is precisely through this "psychic shorthand" and "telescoping" that he created images "deep" enough to hold and express his protagonist's primordial identity. Delmore Schwartz addressed this quality of psychic depth in Roethke with great insight when he noted: "The reader who supposes that Roethke is really a primitive lyric poet loses or misses a great deal. Perhaps the best way to describe what is under the surface is to quote Valéry's remark that the nervous system is the greatest of all poems."[4]

Thus Bly's insistence that deep images unlock the unconscious mind was a discovery Roethke had made in the mid forties in the first four "lost son" poems. During the late fifties and early sixties, Bly would advocate a poetry that transcended the constraints of the human ego and allowed man to participate *with* nature and be at home in the universe. Calling for an alternative to the cerebrally oriented and rationally enclosed literature characteristic of writers like Lowell, Arthur Miller, and Saul Bellow, Bly singled out only Walt Whitman and Roethke as American poets who have brought us "news of the universe."[5] Bly's belief that deep images lead us back to the primary connections between the human self and the animistic world was in some way an emanation of Roethke's poetics of two decades earlier. For Roethke had created a sacred and numinous nature and an archetypal mind that embodied what Bly later called a "poetry that reaches out in waves over everything that is alive."[6] Bly was advocating what Roethke had accomplished in *The Lost Son:* a poetry that was aesthetically and ontologically organic—free of a dualistic human identity. Perhaps no protagonist in American poetry learns to overcome the dualisms of the Western rational mind with more happy passion than the lost son, who cries at the closing of "A Field of Light":

My heart lifted up with the great grasses;
The weeds believed me, and the nesting birds.

4. Delmore Schwartz, *Selected Essays*, eds. Donald A. Dike and David H. Zucker (Chicago, 1970), 187.
5. Robert Bly, "The Dead World and the Live World," *Sixties*, VIII (1966), 2.
6. *Ibid.*

There were clouds making a rout of shapes crossing a windbreak of
   cedars,
And a bee shaking drops from a rain-soaked honeysuckle.
The worms were delighted as wrens.
And I walked, I walked through the light air;
I moved with the morning.

Roethke is not a projectivist in the post-Poundian way that Charles
Olson lays out in his famous "Projectivist Verse" essay. Roethke's
sense of form and intent is different from that of poets like Robert
Duncan, Robert Creeley, and Denise Levertov. However, his kinetic
language, his bardic feeling about the spoken quality of the poem,
and his organic and dynamic concept of consciousness dovetail with
the forms of inclusive openness that Olson and the Black Mountain
poets would be practicing and preaching by the early fifties.
Roethke, who was older than Olson, shared one major source of
influence with him—William Carlos Williams. The impact of
Williams on Roethke accounts for some of the kinetic language and
protean form in the "lost son" poems, and several of the poetic
principles that Olson would advocate in his 1950 projectivist verse
manifesto had, in the "lost son" sequence, already become second
nature for Roethke, who wrote with both the compulsive contain-
ment of a metaphysical and the discursive openness of a Poundian.

Many of the essential ideas in Olson's projectivist essay indicate
the degree to which Roethke's experiments intersect with the Black
Mountain orientation. Olson calls for a "revolution of the ear" and
"the *kinetics* of the thing." "The poem itself must," he says, "at all
points, be a high energy construct," for "it is from the union of the
mind and the ear that the syllable is born." For Olson, the poem has
to unite linguistic rhythms with physiological rhythms, and he in-
sists that "verse will only do in which a poet manages to register
both the acquisitions of his ear and the pressures of his breath."

Olson's idea of organic free verse form leads him to think of the
poem as a field in which the words that embody objects create a
"necessary series of tensions." In this dynamic idea of form it is
essential that the poet not dissipate his linguistic energy in any
way. "The descriptive functions generally have to be watched,
every second, in projective verse, because of their easiness, and

thus their drain on the energy which composition by field allows into a poem. *Any* slackness takes off attention, that crucial thing, from the job at hand." The kinetic field, Olson believes, is shaped to a large degree by the relationship between linguistic sound and the movement of the poet's consciousness. Thus the poet can, "without the convention of rime and meter, record the listening he has done to his own speech." And the success of such an effort rests largely with the ear—"the ear, the ear which has collected, which has listened, the ear, which is so close to the mind that it is the mind's, that it has the mind's speed." This dynamic kind of poetic language, Olson believes, could carry the kind of energy poetry has not "carried in our language since the Elizabethans."[7]

Roethke's own breakthrough to the principles of organic form occurred, of course, in the forties when he began working on *The Lost Son*. In a letter he wrote to Williams while he was at work on the poem "The Lost Son," he proclaims an idea of dynamic poetic speech that sounds a good bit like Olson. He has written a poem, he says, "for the ear and not the eye. . . with the mood or the action on the page, not talked about, not the meditative, T. S. Eliot kind of thing" (SL, 122). This letter and the others Roethke exchanged with Williams in the forties reveal his enthusiasm for Williams' idea of organic form. Thus, in a historical sense Williams becomes a common source for Roethke and Olson.

A comic aphorism Roethke recorded in a notebook of the mid-forties indicates how deeply he felt about the importance of the ear: "All ear and no brain / Makes Teddy inane" (SF, 15). Like Olson, Roethke has no use for slackness or lack of linguistic pressure. His notebook entries of the mid-forties stress his commitment to a dynamic and organic free verse, and, like Olson, he complains that "so much of modern verse seems tensionless" (SF, 176). Although Roethke was not a theorist as Olson was, his belief that if the poet "can't make the words move, he has nothing" (SF, 172), is similar to Olson's advocacy of dynamic language in an open field. In discussing the influences on the "lost son" poems, Roethke points to "German and English folk literature, particularly Mother Goose; Eliz-

7. Charles Olson, "Projective Verse," in *The New American Poetry*, ed. Donald Allen (New York, 1960), 386–97.

abethan and Jacobean drama, especially the songs and rants" (PC, 41). Oddly enough, but not coincidentally, we find Roethke and Olson both appealing to the dynamism of Elizabethan English in their desire to reclaim some original energy for contemporary free verse.

In his desire to write "a poem that is the shape of the psyche under great stress," Roethke created an organic form that flexed its syntax. The protean shape of the lost son's mind is, to a large degree, generated in the euphonic qualities of Roethke's ear which in turn shape the kinetic force of the line. The dimensions of the lost son's psychic experience create—in the most organic way—the stresses in the lines and the nature of the lines that constitute the stanzas in the four lost son poems. Like Olson, Roethke disdains artificial syntactic connectives and the use of traditional metaphor and simile. His goal is to create a language that embodies in every aspect of its form the content of the mind. That moment of manic frenzy in section 3 of "The Lost Son"—which is followed by the two lines made up of "money" and "water" that disclose the matter-spirit duality in the protagonist—exemplifies this kind of protean organicism.

> All the windows are burning! What's left of my life?
> I want the old rage, the lash of primordial milk!
> Goodbye, goodbye, old stones, the time-order is going,
> I have married my hands to perpetual agitation,
> I run, I run to the whistle of money.
>
> Money money money
> water water water

A poet of consequence to the evolving direction of his art is naturally a beneficiary of a given moment in history. As a poet coming to maturity in the waning phase of modernism, Roethke was able to have a perspective on that great generation. He could make selective use of the innovations of the period and absorb what he had to of writers like Eliot, Stevens, Williams, James Joyce, and William Faulkner—to name several who influenced him. Unlike poets of the generation to follow him, who often felt antagonistic about the modernist masters, Roethke felt both connected to and yet, I think, shrewdly distanced from the age of Eliot and Pound.

Roethke's maturation during the middle decade of the century gave him a healthy and creative perspective on modernism as well as a broad cultural vantage point. For as a mid-century American poet, he was able to bring together—to synthesize in his idiosyncratic way—dominant post-Christian intellectual movements: Romanticism, Darwinism, and modern psychology (Freudian and Jungian). Roethke had enough historical distance from these intellectual world views to be able to create out of them a set of assumptions and ultimately an aesthetic myth from which his language and poetic concerns could evolve.

Critics have examined at length the importance of British Romanticism, American Transcendentalism, and Freudian and Jungian psychology in Roethke's work. But Roethke's organic aestheticism is also, at least in part, an emanation of Darwinism. He is, of course, in no way a Darwinist; in the obvious sense, he is neither secular nor deterministic. Rather, proceeding from certain Darwinian assumptions, he extends his own version of what can be called post-Darwinian myth. Darwin's organic conception of life, growth, and evolution, and his idea of an organic architecture unifying the entire scheme of plant and animal life, had immense meaning for Roethke. His ability to identify with the subhuman world of plants, stones, and microorganisms in *The Lost Son* and *Praise To The End!*, his assertion in "The Waking" that "the lowly worm climbs up a winding stair," and his sense of phylogenetic origins in "The Far Field," where we find him "Fingering a shell, / Thinking: / Once I was something like this, mindless, / Or perhaps with another mind, less peculiar," exemplify how thoroughly he absorbed a vision of the Darwinian cosmos.

Viewing Roethke from the vantage point of the century's final decade, one might say that he pioneered our first important postmodernist poems. In creating a mythic autobiography out of his vision of certain intersecting intellectual forces that shaped America at mid-century, he was able to find a relationship between an idea of the transcendent, a modern notion of the natural world, and a concept of the contemporary human self. In forming a new script from the intellectual realms his imagination filtered to the supple language of his rhetoric, the greenhouse keeper's son and the spiritually a.iven manic-depressive poet forged our first contemporary confessional persona.

It is important to keep in mind that behind these three modern intellectual trends lies Roethke's idiosyncratic but deep commitment to a Judeo-Christian tradition. The more orthodox idea of God that he presents in his final group of poems, "A Sequence, Sometimes Metaphysical," discloses a persistent sense of otherness—a pre-Romantic sense of the separateness that exists between man and God—which is evident at various points in various forms throughout Roethke's poetry. His interest in Christian mysticism, his use of mystical ideas and tropes, and his thorough reading of Evelyn Underhill's *Mysticism* underscore this dimension in Roethke's work. Numerous notebook entries reveal Roethke's spiritual zeal, among them "Those damned old mystics have got me despising myself" (SF, 218), and "If God does not exist, neither do we" (SF, 219).

Finally, this Judeo-Christian aspect of Roethke's art in no way contradicts or adds confusion to the modern sensibility he created out of Romanticism, Darwinism, modern psychology, and literary modernism. That his Judeo-Christian strain could be also an integral part of his vision is a testimony not only to his genius but to the largeness of his poetry and the permanence of the myth he made for our time—a myth he created out of both his personal past and our cultural past.

ONE

Opening House

It is not only in retrospect that the title of Roethke's first book of poems, *Open House* (1941), is an appropriate metaphor for the formal beginning of his career. The forty-five poems in *Open House* which, with the help of close friends Stanley Kunitz, Rolfe Humphries, and Louise Bogan, Roethke carefully chose and arranged, are the culmination of twelve years of serious writing. They are the poems he considered to be the most representative of his concerns as well as his finest poetic achievements.

It is telling that the critics have been far less generous to the volume than the initial reviewers were. To some degree this is endemic to the act of literary criticism, for in evaluating the body of a writer's work one must make judgments and compare and contrast the various phases of the literary career. And in contrast with the achievement of the poetry which follows, *Open House* has its limitations. The magnitude of Roethke's ensuing poetic career has forced critics to consider the first volume in light of *The Lost Son, Praise to the End!, The Waking, Words for the Wind*, and *The Far Field*. Consequently, many recent critical treatments of *Open House* have distorted and overlooked elements in the poems which must be understood if Roethke's first book is to be adequately appreciated.

For the most part, *Open House* received favorable reviews from some formidable poets and critics. W. H. Auden enthusiastically noted in *Saturday Review of Literature*: "To remember and to transform the humiliation into something beautiful, as Mr. Roethke does, is rare. Every one of the lyrics in this book, whether serious or light, shares the same kind of ordered sensibility: *Open House* is completely successful." Yvor Winters remarked that "Roethke is ashamed neither of having subject matter nor of the kind of subject matter he has, and he writes in a style that is good in this period and would be good in any other." In a review in the Boston *Evening Transcript*, John Holmes said, "The wholeness of *Open House* demands comment. Mr. Roethke has built it with infinite patience in five sections." Commenting on the distinctiveness of his talent, Elizabeth Drew in *Atlantic Monthly* praised Roethke for "the sense of inner security and certainty which his poems communicate. . . . his poems have a controlled grace of movement. . . . he attains an austerity of contemplation and a pared, spare strictness of language very unusual in poets of today."[1] I do not want to pretend to ignore literary history and treat the volume as if it were more than a solid but modest beginning. Yet, I would like to treat *Open House* as freshly as possible, not apologizing for its shortcomings and failures but rather accepting it on its own ground.

In evaluating *Open House*, it is important to realize that two strains of sensibility run through the volume; one is essentially romantic and the other primarily metaphysical, neither is completely separate from the other, yet neither is fused with the other as in the later poems.[2] The poems that reveal Roethke's romantic disposition, such as "Night Journey," "Slow Season," and "The Coming of the Cold," find a pure and noble condition in nature and deal with a fluxional relationship between the spirit and nature, between organic process and consciousness.

Even a critic as fine as Jay Parini, who argues that the poems in

1. W. H. Auden, "Verse and the Times," *Saturday Review of Literature*, XVIII (April 5, 1941), 30–31; Yvor Winters, "The Poems of Theodore Roethke," *Kenyon Review*, III (Autumn, 1941), 514–16; John Holmes, "Poems and Things," Boston *Evening Transcript*, March 24, 1941, p. 9; Elizabeth Drew, "Bookshelf," *Atlantic Monthly*, CLXVIII (August, 1941).

2. Richard Allen Blessing in *Theodore Roethke's Dynamic Vision* (Bloomington, Ind., 1974), 40, refers to *Open House* as a failed book because of the disparity between what the book's title suggests and what the poems actually are; Jenijoy La Belle in *The Echoing Wood of Theodore Roethke* (Princeton, N.J., 1976), 7, calls Roethke in *Open House* a frightened imitator; Rosemary Sullivan in *Theodore Roethke: The Garden Master* (Seattle, 1975), 19, also sees him as a borrower and imitator; and Mary Hayden in "*Open House*: Poetry of the Constricted Self," *Northwest Review*, XI (Summer, 1971), 119, misses the metaphysical nature of the poetry and maintains that the poems are flawed, cryptic, and disjunctive.

Open House may be metaphysical in style but are essentially roman-tic in theme, does not allow for the full success of the metaphysical style Roethke executed.[3] The technique, perception, and experience in poems like "My Dim-Wit Cousin," "For an Amorous Lady," "The Auction," "Sale," "Highway: Michigan," "No Bird," to name sev-eral, are not romantic in form or content. In these poems Roethke makes use of familiar metaphysical conventions: the conceit, wit, paradox, irony, and a more formal metrics. He "strives to concep-tualize his sensations and materialize his concepts,"[4] to have, as Eliot says, "the intellect at the tip of his senses."[5] Furthermore, the metaphysical method proceeds through the poet's act of condensing images and metaphors, so that by the "choice of contrasts descrip-tion is abbreviated, narration quickened and analysis strength-ened."[6] (This condensation and compression naturally created in Roethke's metaphysical poems the very effect some of his critics labeled a failure.) In addition, poems such as "Highway: Michigan," "Ballad of the Clairvoyant Widow," and "The Auction" criticize life with a corrective irony characteristic of the metaphysical poet's wit.

If "the characteristic mood of metaphysical verse is recognized by its repeatedly sardonic quality, restless disillusionments, irritable surfaces and stinging effects—and its terrible intuitions,"[7] one might well expect a poet who in part nursed on Henry Vaughan, John Donne, and George Herbert and who greatly admired his met-aphysical friends, Stanley Kunitz and Elinor Wylie, to express his anguish in a compressed and controlled manner. Finally, the meta-physical poems in *Open House* evince "thought that is in control" and "images that are no more than apt illustrations of thought"—phrases Hyatt Waggoner uses in describing the metaphysical tem-perament in Emily Dickinson but applicable as well to one strain in *Open House*.[8]

In short, to appreciate the merits of *Open House* it is necessary to accept some of the metaphysical premises from which Roethke oper-

3. Jay Parini, *Theodore Roethke: An American Romantic* (Amherst, Mass., 1979).
4. Sona Raiziss, *The Metaphysical Passion* (Philadelphia, 1952), 28.
5. T. S. Eliot, *Selected Essays* (New York, 1964).
6. Raiziss, *The Metaphysical Passion*, 31.
7. *Ibid.*, 56.
8. Hyatt H. Waggoner, *American Visionary Poetry* (Baton Rouge, 1982), 212.

ated. This is not to overlook the shortcomings of the volume; he was not writing a neo-metaphysical poetry of the rank and order of Louise Bogan or John Crowe Ransom. *Open House* has its limitations indeed. Some of the poetry is overtly self-conscious, awkward, and stiff; at times Roethke's poetic sources are not well assimilated, and his formal meter can be artificial. Yet one must look at the book through the disposition of its maker at the time he made it, not in contrast with the different kind of poetry into which he grew. Later Roethke would be able to bring together his metaphysical temperament with an organic free verse form and visionary sensibility; here he is still testing his ground.

The title resonates with meaning both for the poems within the volume and for the aspirations of a young poet at the beginning of his journey. The metaphoric dimension of the book's title has an ontological and spiritual meaning. "To keep open house with one's heart"—the phrase is Nietzsche's and Roethke might well have known it—is fundamental to Roethke's essential way of knowing reality and measuring truth. The title proclaims the need to search the self for the truth and echoes the sentiment of Christ's "and to him that Knocketh it shall be opened" (Matt. 7:8). The title also celebrates a poet's beginning; the opening of the house is the self through which the spirit seeks, the heart feels, and the imagination begins to burn. Roethke knew Emerson's essay *Nature,* and whether or not it was in his conscious mind during the years he was completing his book, the closing words of the essay illuminate greatly the meaning of a young poet opening house: "Every spirit builds itself a house, and beyond its house a world, and beyond its world a heaven. Know that the world exists for you. For you is the phenomenon perfect. What we are, that only we can see. All that Adam had, all that Caesar could, you have and can do. Adam called his house heaven and earth; Caesar called his house Rome. . . . Build therefore your own world."[9]

Woven throughout the book's five sections are poems that fall into three categories: poems concerned with the process of poetic

9. Ralph Waldo Emerson, *The Selected Writings,* ed. Brooks Atkinson (New York, 1950), 42.

knowing and imagination; poems dealing with the meaning of the past—the poet's family life and the middle-class world of Saginaw, Michigan; and poems exploring the dimensions of the natural world. Taken as a whole, the book reveals a poet exploring the sources of his world—searching the rooms of his parents' house, observing nature, criticizing the social world of his youth, and making inquiry into the mysterious process of poetry and the substance of the imagination.

The opening poem, "Open House," is an overture to the essential ways of knowing and feeling, being and expressing that will come to define Roethke's distinctive disposition. The regular meter, *a b a b c c*, of the three sextains compresses the poet's emotion. At certain moments when Roethke departs from the predictable end rhyming, the regular meter becomes a counterpoise to the off rhyme and generates a quality of surprise and dissonance which effectively creates a sense of anguish and struggle. The self is the house which must be kept open, for the poet's responsibility is to feel the "secrets" of self-knowledge:

> My secrets cry aloud.
> I have no need for tongue.
> My heart keeps open house,
> My doors are widely swung.
> An epic of the eyes
> My love, with no disguise.

Each stanza intensifies the experience. We move from emotion and love through truth and nakedness to anger and rage. Because poetry for Roethke is self-revelatory and prophetic, it involves struggle and pain. Like Whitman, Roethke must become "undisguised and naked." For nakedness, which is paradoxically vulnerability and protection ("I'm naked to the bone, / With nakedness my shield"), is the only way the poet can transform self-knowledge into universal truth. As was true for his transcendental forefathers, Roethke believes that to wear the self representatively the poet must "keep the spirit spare." In a way that Emerson and Whitman proclaimed a century earlier, the true poet must not simply be a versifier, but a seer, a maker of Truth. Even this early, what Kenneth Burke would later refer to as Roethke's "search for a . . . purified speech"[10] is essential to the young poet who insists that "the deed will speak the truth / In language strict and pure."

In several poems Roethke explores the nature of this "rage" which "warps" his "clearest cry." The time of creative barrenness is equated with death in "Death Piece." And the imagination, in the poet's struggle with inertia, is likened to an abandoned beehive, "sealed honey-tight." In stasis, creative energy becomes motion incapable of movement. The paradoxical conceit of the mind as a "curving prow / Of motion moored to rock" creates the immense frustration of creative energy, stalled yet indomitable.

Roethke constantly conceives of the imagination as something impenetrable, pure, and ultimately inscrutable. In "The Adamant," the enduring substance of the imagination—"the true substance"— cannot be undone by reason. The rational mind is seen as a machine whose mechanical process is inimical to the intuitive knowing of poetry.

> The teeth of knitted gears
> Turn slowly through the night,
> But the true substance bears
> The hammer's weight.

For Roethke the center holds; "Compression cannot break / A center so congealed." He imagines the source of poetry as an encased force inside the mind. He refers to it in "Reply to Censure" as the place of "dignity within, / And quiet at the core." In "The Adamant," this diamond-hard center remains unyielding and pure: "The tool can chip no flake: / The core lies sealed."

More dramatically, " 'Long Live the Weeds' " embodies the poet's situation and the imagination's insistent irrationality. The weeds are the wild, unkept vegetation, and they become for the poet an elemental force—his flowers of chaos. Like the weeds, the poet grows in those places where most cannot: "The bitter rock, the barren soil / That force the son of man to toil." The allusion to Ezekiel, and to Christ, the Son of man, identifies the poet both with the weeds which live in marginal places and with the outcasts who live there

10. Kenneth Burke, "The Vegetal Radicalism of Theodore Roethke," *Sewanee Review*, LXVIII (Winter, 1950), 76.

too in order to find truth. What the rational mind deems unholy and ugly the poetic mind and the spirit embrace as purifying.

> All things unholy, marred by curse,
> The ugly of the universe.
> The rough, the wicked, and the wild
> That keep the spirit undefiled.

Roethke's weeds, like Williams' saxifrage—that rock breaker in "A Sort of a Song"—are tough and durable as the poet must be and, like the imagination, are endlessly resourceful in their ability to grow. The meaning of the "weeds" suggests something about the poet's struggle to live. In order to "hope, love, create, or drink and die" the sacred disorder of the weeds must prevail. " 'Long Live the Weeds,' " is, however, a good example of Roethke's inability to reconcile his romantic and metaphysical impulses. The poem, which celebrates the imagination's creative chaos, closes with a stilted, formal, and abstract ending (not good metaphysical execution) that contradicts the meaning of the poem and detracts from its effectiveness.

Although the ultimate workings of poetic perception remain mysterious, Roethke probes the process of seeing. In "The Signals," the physical eye and the mind's eye work together. As the "known particulars" of the quotidian world "dart across a corner of the eye," a process speeds up which transforms optical seeing into imaginative seeing. Roethke imagines images that "flicker faster than a blue-tailed swift" and then almost disappear in a momentary void "when dark follows dark in lightning rift" (an image that even suggests the void in the beginning of the creation myth in Genesis). Yet this deep perception remains elusive, and the poet "cannot put . . . [his] glance upon them tight." What he cannot know perceptually he can at least sense with "the blood"—his elemental being.

The infrangible center of the mind in "The Unextinguished" is also a region where being and creation are inseparable. Like Dickinson, who, breaking through to the liberating region of the mind, felt a "Funeral" in her "Brain," Roethke, working from the conceit of a sunset, sees a "conflagration in the upper air." There is a corresponding light in the upper regions of the mind. The "fire of heaven" becomes a smoldering potency in the dream mind of sleep.

In the somnolent mind the waking imagination returns to some reservoir in the brain and burns "backward to a blackened heap"— that archetypal space which Roethke would later call in "Night Crow" a "moonless black, / Deep in the brain, far back." Again, at the mind's core the active imagination persists. What the mind sees in the waking light is nurtured in some dark cavern of the imagination and is reactivated by a "morning light" which "pokes the crumbled coal the ashes hid" and stirs the febrile passion of poetry with an intenser heat "until thought crackles white across the brain."

However, Roethke's understanding of imagination and the workings of poetry is not defined solely by a need to apprehend sensuously the processes of mind. He conceives of imagination and poetry as having an integral and organic relation with being in the most physiological sense. Poetry is, for him, as necessary as flesh and blood. Anatomical metaphors constantly define the relationship between the poet and his utterance. In "The Signals" and "The Unextinguished," the process of seeing involves the eye "lid"—a particular physiological mechanism. In "Death Piece," the fabric of poetry and the fiber of the self are inseparable—"Invention sleeps within a skull" and emptiness is felt in "every cell." The imagined elemental energy in "Genesis" returns to the body so that a "river's leaping source / Is locked in narrow bone." Biochemistry and metaphysics are in constant interaction: "wisdom" which "floods the mind, / Invades quiescent blood"; even "sense" is a "secretion" from "a pearl within the brain."

In poems that seem to espouse a body-soul dualism, Roethke is finally unable to renounce the body. In "Epidermal Macabre" he wishes to dispense with the flesh that houses the "false accouterments of sense" but imagines himself in a Whitmanesque way, paradoxically, as "a most / Incarnadine and carnal ghost." Or, in "Silence," the anguish and struggle of living and creating are united with the poet's physical being: "The tight nerves leading to the throat" withhold the poet's grief, and unrequited emotion "shakes . . . [his] skull to disrepair."

If the poems that concern themselves with poetry, imagination, and the mind mark Roethke's growth toward aesthetic understanding and artistic awareness, the poems that present his confrontations with his family's past and the middle-class world of Saginaw in which he grew up define a further aspect of the young poet forging an identity. In a Hawthornian sense, "Feud" is a poet's quarrel with man's fallen condition and a confrontation with the tainted legacy of the human past and one's ancestral inheritance. As if aware of Original Sin for the first time, Roethke, "Recoiling from the serpent head / Of fate . . . blubber[s] in surprise." With an atavistic sense, he calls himself a "Darling of an infected brood" and feels "disaster climb the vein." "The light essential" is oppressed by an ominous past of "dark forms" and "Old secrets." Reconciled to the impossibility of recovering a prelapsarian world, the best the poet can do is penitence to purify the self, to keep the spirit spare: "This ancient feud / Is seldom won. The spirit starves / Until the dead have been subdued."

Implicit in the "dark forms" and "infected brood" of this poem and the uneasy mood in the other family poems is the Roethke family tragedy. Friction between his father and his Uncle Charlie came to a head in 1922 when Roethke was fourteen. Roethke explained the feud in a short story he wrote in college. The two brothers, Otto and Charlie, were co-owners of the greenhouse; Uncle Charlie deceived Otto, worked little, and extorted money from the business. Unable to tolerate such behavior, Otto sold his half of the business to Uncle Charlie, who proved incapable of running it and committed suicide. Two months later, Otto died of colon cancer. These events hitting Roethke at this vulnerable age no doubt left him with a complex feeling about inheriting the sins of his fathers.

In "The Auction," the poet more effectively cleans house and purges himself of the ancestral past. In order to open his own house, he must leave behind his father's house. In a dreamlike way, Roethke returns home to find an auctioneer on his front lawn selling his outgrown youthful emotions.

> "One coat of pride, perhaps a bit threadbare;
> Illusion's trinkets, splendid for the young;
> Some items, miscellaneous, marked 'Fear';
> The chair of honor, with a missing rung."

It becomes a poem of purgation and hope. As his "spirits rose each time the hammer fell," he is able to sever ties with youth and leaves "home with unencumbered will." With "all the rubbish of confusion sold," the poet can start out on his own, less hampered by the fears and illusions of his youth. In many ways "The Auction" is an early version of the kind of liberation Roethke later experiences in "Child on Top of a Greenhouse."

Although "Sale" continues the poet's struggle to leave behind his family and the home of his youth, the poem assumes a more social tone. In fact, its invective against the middle-class life of his parents and their Prussian fastidiousness reminds one of Henry Miller's loathing for his Nordic ancestors and his insistence that their obsessions with cleanliness and order were crimes against the soul: "Never once had they opened the door which leads to the soul; never once did they dream of taking a blind leap into the dark. After dinner the dishes were promptly washed and put in the closet; after the paper was read it was neatly folded and laid on the shelf. . . . Everything was for tomorrow, but tomorrow never came."[11] In a haunting way, each of Roethke's quatrains with its perfect rhymes conveys the monotony of this kind of world. Here the feud is familial, the estate tainted with bad blood; it is a house of misplaced values and emotional death. The poet orders everything sold—"The what-not, the settee, the Chippendale chairs." Each catalog of items sold has its corresponding emotional equivalents so that "an attic of horrors, a closet of fears," the "fume of decay," and "grandfather's sinister hovering hand" are all a "taint in a blood that was running too thin." The poet's only recourse is to free himself by leaving everything behind; he must sell it all, from "The furniture polished and polished so grand" to "The antimacassar for the sofa in red."

Indeed, the poem takes on the tone of the sort of middle-class satire that characterized the Dutch genre paintings of Jan Steen or Adrian Van Ostade. Roethke is contemptuous of his Philistine family which uses the library as a "card room instead" and prefers a sentimental portrait of "some watery eyes in a Copley head." Forced to recognize some ultimate condition in this banal reality, Roethke concludes that a world this passionless and barren is a world "encrusted with sin."

11. Henry Miller, *Tropic of Cancer* (New York, 1961), xiii.

In the two poems that follow, "Highway: Michigan" and "Idyll," he continues to upbraid the ways of the middle class and takes, what is rare for him, a vaguely political stance. For Roethke the commuter traffic jam is the condition of modern alienated man. No believer in progress, Roethke surveys the "progress of the jaded" automobile factory workers. Like D. H. Lawrence before him, he sees humanity imprisoned by society's technological scheme; without any human relation to their work, the workers are "the prisoners of speed / Who flee in what their hands have made." In Roethke's infernal vision of mechanized modernity, near death by machine marks modern man's doom. From out of the car accident "One driver, pinned beneath the seat, / Escapes from the machine at last." In this sense, he is closer to Eliot than he is to Williams or Hart Crane, about whom Roethke writes: "Crane's assumption: the machine is important; we must put it in our lives, make it part of our imaginative life. Answer: the hell it is. An ode to an icebox is possible, since it contains fruit and meat" (SF, 239).

With none of the New Dealer's liberal faith in science and technology, progress, bigness, and bureaucracy, Roethke was, as his graduate school acquaintance Kenneth Porter called him, "a good-natured conservative."[12] In "Idyll," suburbia is modern man's condition of quiet desperation, a kind of death in life where "darkness creeps up on the well-groomed" town. It is a world of dull-mindedness and ignorance where everyone is cut off from both human reality and nature. "We sit in the porch swing, content and half asleep," says the poet, "indifferent . . . to the nestling's last peep" and "Unmindful of terror and headlines, of speeches and guns."

"The Premonition," "The Reminder," and "On the Road to Woodlawn" are childhood recollections of the poet's father and the greenhouse. Walking along the riverbank with his father in "The Premonition," he recalls his father dipping "his hand in the shallow." Roethke is able to seize this detail and intensify it into a moment of perception that signifies something greater: "Water ran over and under / Hair on a narrow wrist bone." The afterimage that follows the poet becomes a premonition of his father's death and a

12. Kenneth Porter, "Roethke at Harvard, 1930–1931 and the Decade After," *Northwest Review,* XI (Summer, 1971), 142.

baptism into the water of mortality. In a ghostly way, his father's face is "lost in a maze of water."

The image of his father as horticulturist and greenhouse keeper haunts Roethke even this early. In "On the Road to Woodlawn" and "The Reminder" loss and nostalgia dominate the poet's mood.

> I miss the polished brass, the powerful black horses,
> The drivers creaking the seats of the baroque hearses,
> The high-piled floral offerings and sentimental verses,
> The carriages reeking with varnish and stale perfume.
> ("On the Road to Woodlawn")

Since funerals are a large part of a florist's business (occasions bringing prosperity for the greenhouse owner), he remembers the ceremoniousness of the funeral with excitement. He is still an innocent in this poem, unlike in "The Premonition" and "The Reminder." The father is the implicit hero, the supplier of the "high-piled floral offerings," and the young Roethke's ticket to the event. The poem's lyric impressionism and faithful observation and recollection separate it from the predominant metaphysical style of the book. In this sense all three of these poems look forward to the greenhouse poems.

Although "The Reminder" is formal in its rhyming quatrains, the quotidian detail in the poem gives it a sense of the organic that characterizes the greenhouse world.

> I remember the crossing-tender's geranium border
> That blossomed in soot; a black cat licking its paw;
> The bronze wheat arranged in strict and formal order;
> And the precision that for you was ultimate law.

The father with his green thumb is a life force, Godlike here, as Roethke evokes Andrew Marvell's "The Garden": "You wound the watch in an old-fashioned locket / And pulled the green shade against morning sun." The poem closes with the poet grown up, alienated (similar to the closing of "Frau, Frau, Frau"), and cut off from the presence of his father, the creator and Prussian order maker. "In the dirt and disorder I cherish one scrap of illusion / A cheap clock ticking in ghostly cicada voice." Something sinister and surreal emerges in this final moment; the ticking of the clock is time passing but the association of this dissonant sound with the cicada brings him from the confines of his dingy room back to nature. This restores him to a natural world in which his father's presence—no matter how ghostly—still exists.

For Roethke, to write about his childhood is to write about nature. His youth was defined by the fertile Saginaw Valley, which he recalls as still having virgin timber, and, of course, by the twenty-five acres of greenhouses that comprised the family business. His grandfather, William Roethke, who had been Bismarck's head forester before coming to America in the 1870s, began the greenhouses which "became the most extensive in that part of America" (PC, 7–8). Nature was a way of life for the Roethke family. The greenhouses "were to me, I realize now, both heaven and hell, a kind of tropics created in the savage climate of Michigan, where austere German-Americans turned their love of order and their terrifying efficiency into something truly beautiful. It was a universe, several worlds, which, even as a child, one worried about, and struggled to keep alive" (PC, 8–9).

As an adolescent he sensed a correspondence between the natural world and the inner life. In a college essay, "Some Self-Analysis," Roethke echoes Emerson's sentiment that "nature is so pervaded with human life that there is something of humanity in all and in every particular."[13] He exclaims: "I can sense the moods of nature almost instinctively. Ever since I could walk, I have spent as much time as I could in the open. A perception of nature—no matter how delicate, how subtle, how evanescent,—remains with me forever. . . . When I get alone under an open sky where man isn't too evident,—then I'm tremendously exalted and a thousand vivid ideas and sweet visions flood my consciousness" (PC, 4).

In much of *Open House*, nature embodies a fecundity of spirit which is the poet's hope. From the vantage point of her "attic window," the widow muse in "Ballad of the Clairvoyant Widow" finds the legacy of "God's country" to be a dismal reality of bourgeois complacency, intellectual hypocrisy, social injustice, and apocryphal progress. When the young poet asks her if there is any "semblance of that thing called 'Hope'?" she answers:

13. Emerson, *Selected Writings*, 35.

The gulls ride on the water, the gulls have come and gone,
The men on rail and roadway keep moving on and on.

The salmon climb the rivers, the rivers nudge the sea,
The green comes up forever in the fields of our country.

She asserts once more two primary nineteenth-century Romantic notions: the belief that America has an expansive frontier which allows for what Roethke would later call "perpetual journey," and a faith in the primacy of nature. And the widow in this poem looks into the future more clairvoyantly than even Roethke could have imagined; for that place where "the salmon climb the rivers" and "the rivers nudge the sea" is the very Puget Sound where Roethke would live for the last fifteen years of his life and stake his final frontier in the poems of "North American Sequence." For a poet who ceaselessly probes places of juncture where boundaries merge and limits are redefined, the "place, where sea and fresh water meet, / Is important," as Roethke would say later in "The Rose." The illimitable possibility of growth and fertility ("the green comes up forever") is still, Roethke maintains, fundamental to the meaning of America. His "green" echoes, as well, the seminal metaphor of *Leaves of Grass*—that "hopeful green stuff woven" out of which Whitman created the common element that unites all humanity and affirms life's renewing spirit.

More self-consciously than in the greenhouse poems, Roethke focuses on nature's in-between times. In nature's processes of change and transformation, he finds corresponding relationships to the self and the imagination. The anticipation of a storm in "Interlude" returns the poet to a mythic time of first creation. Roethke sees in the storm's imminence the undifferentiated beginning: "The chaos grew as hour by hour the light / Decreased beneath an undivided sky." Although the supernatural light of creation ignites the inner light of imagination, the storm's failure to climax leaves the poet, in a sense, betrayed, suspended between expectation and stasis. Paradoxically, "The wind lay motionless in the long grass." The unconsummated event in nature undercuts any possibility of transcendent experience for the poet.

The year's decline from fertility to decay is the in-between time of "Slow Season." Keats's "Ode to Autumn" and Frost's "After Apple

Picking" seem to stand behind the poem. Roethke enters a Keatsian world of "mists and mellow fruitfulness" where, at the juncture of ripeness and decay, the poet eases into a somnolent state of mind. In this time of "drowsing off," as Frost says, the self turns inward to the fecund imagination. For Roethke this slowing time involves a transformation of the self and an altered sense of time: "The haze of harvest drifts along the field / Until clear eyes put on the look of sleep." Although the poet must reorient himself in a way that involves his entire being—"blood," "breath," and "eyes"—the dimensions of this wakeful sleep remain unexplored, and the poem ends with a flat, ineffective summary: "Our vernal wisdom moves through ripe to sere."

In "The Coming of the Cold," Roethke displays the acute awareness of nature that heralds the distinctiveness of his perception in many of his later poems. In this transitional time, Roethke explores the meaning of the whole within the delicate particulars. All of the senses absorb the changing season: "The plum drops pitch upon the ground, / And nostrils widen as they pass . . . The dill bears up its acrid crown." Although the relationship between the self and nature is somewhat static here, a kind of cataloguing self-effacement looks forward to the great poems of "North American Sequence."

"In Praise of Prairie" continues to proclaim the indigenous territory of America, a version of that noble landscape which Emerson says "conspires with the spirit to emancipate us."[14] As Bryant in his poem "The Prairies" sings the praise of "The unshorn fields, boundless, and beautiful" and hails the sublime dimension of America's native ground. Roethke also finds in this expansive space a sense of freedom. This illimitable horizon transforms the relationship between the self and the cosmos: "Our feet are sometimes level with the sky, / When we are walking on a treeless plain." Geographic expanse and the self's creative topography merge and define the poet in an open world.

Perhaps more than any other poem in *Open House*, "Night Journey," which I consider the finest poem in the collection, points the way to what is to come. It joins Roethke's epical sense of America as

14. *Ibid.*, 28.

an unexplored territory with a visionary process of seeing which affirms that journeying is an experience of self-discovery. As the "train bears west," the rocking rhythm both wakes the poet into seeing in the dark and lulls his imagination into wakeful sleep. Perceiving the world from a moving vehicle in the night activates the imagination's transforming power; seeing in the dark is essential to the poet's ability to make metaphor and meaning. In this continuity of knowing, mind and landscape are inseparable.

> Bridges of iron lace,
> A suddenness of trees,
> A lap of mountain mist
> All cross my line of sight,
> Then a bleak wasted place,
> And a lake below my knees.

Roethke's experience is visionary here because the larger imaginative vision grows out of the poet's faithful act of perceiving what is out there in the dark. Such an act involves an entirety of being that is at once visual, imaginative, psychological, and spiritual. "My muscles move with steel, / I wake in every nerve," the poet cries. All levels of reality are brought together through body and mind moving with the vehicle through space. The deep seeing of the imagination is never separated from the motion of the train, and everything assumes an organic doubleness of meaning and vision, as the "double glass" suggests. The "beacon" swinging from "dark to blazing bright" is the mind's eye as well as the train's light.

We are left traveling through the American night on a journey that opens up a limitless expanse for the poet. Although Roethke resolves the poem with a definitive emotion, "I stay up half the night / To see the land I love," the implications of the poem are limitless, the meaning of the journey ongoing. Roethke no doubt made "Night Journey" the final poem in the collection not only because he considered it one of his best poems to date, but also because it summed up some of his largest concerns and foreshadowed things to come. The poem looks forward to the open-endedness that later characterizes *Praise to the End!* and "North American Sequence."

TWO

A Poet's Breakthrough

Between the 1941 publication of *Open House* and about 1946, when most of the poems that would be included in *The Lost Son and Other Poems* (1948) were finished, Theodore Roethke experienced a personal and artistic growth that marked the birth of a major poet. During the early forties he grew into the qualities that would come to define the quintessential nature of his craft and vision. As with American writers like Walt Whitman, Herman Melville, and William Faulkner, who underwent vast transformations in their literary development in short periods of time, it is difficult to see in Roethke's early work the nature of genius that would characterize his mature work.

The self-discovery that defines the period between his first and second books was the beginning of Roethke's uncovering his "existential core," to use a phrase of Stanley Kunitz's.[1] For Roethke, this involved both finding a literary voice and having the psychological self-awareness and emotional courage to wrestle with the primal realities of his past and the often painful traumas of his present. The achievement of the greenhouse poems and the "lost son" sequence has much to do with the fact that Roethke's personal and poetic growth were so well united. His spiritual growth—which enabled him to search the mythic turf of his childhood and face the meaning of his adult mental crises and manic-depressive cycles—was paralleled by a corresponding change in his understanding of poetics.

The years between the publication of *Open House* and *The Lost Son* were filled with a sense of creative euphoria as well as mental tur-

1. "Interview with Stanley Kunitz" in *Columbia* (Fall, 1977), 5.

moil. Allan Seager notes that following the reviews of *Open House* Roethke lapsed into one of his "characteristic periods of dissatisfaction."[2] He often complained that his abilities went unrecognized at Penn State where he was teaching. However, the critical success of his first book was not the only reason he felt dissatisfied with his teaching position; he also sensed that he had come to the end of a phase of writing and personal growth and needed to move on.

One significant manifestation of Roethke's growth, transition, and restless sense of a new beginning can be seen in his new working methods. During these years he began to create the first of the voluminous notebooks that stand behind the poetry he would later publish. The notebooks, at times brilliant poetry themselves, are an extraordinary record of a poet's journey. As Seager recalls, in the thirties Roethke's method of composition was conventional; he would work out a plan for a poem in an orderly and somewhat schematic way, always working on a single poem at a time.[3] Although his notebooks of the late thirties reveal a slight departure from this rigid process of writing, it was not until about 1943, as the notebooks in *Straw for the Fire* document, that Roethke's method of composition and his concept of poetry began to change radically.

The notebooks of the early forties, as Wagoner has presented them, reveal a poet in the throes of self-discovery and artistic awakening. They become the embodiment of a man who was learning, as Roethke later said, that "to go forward (as spiritual man) it is necessary first to go back" (SL, 142). These entries are an organic record of Roethke as a poet, teacher, critic, and spiritually questing man.

The notebooks of the forties show a remarkable sense of creative chaos. They are made up of poem fragments, descriptions of nature, assessments of social situations, parts of letters, critical remarks on contemporary poets, and numerous witty Nietzschean-like aphorisms. Full of self-criticism and self-recognition, the aphorisms reveal Roethke's moments of self-understanding. They disclose a poet on the edge of something new, a poet giving birth to himself, unfurling a poetic temperament and a psychic and spiritual disposition

2. Allan Seager, *The Glass House: The Life of Theodore Roethke* (New York, 1968), 131.
3. *Ibid.*, 131, 161.

that would distinguish his mature work. The somewhat manic, frenzied, and compulsive sense of energy that underscores the notebooks shows us the poet's act of breaking through to something previously unrealized. It might be said that the notebooks reveal Roethke in a phase of individuation.

For Roethke, discovering the essential self involved recovering the past: the personal past of his childhood and the mythical world he later called "the racial memory" (SL, 130). He uses birth metaphors repeatedly and speaks of growth in a procreative, primal way that characterizes what might be called the birth traumas of his inner world. Roethke's self-analysis, reminiscent of the volatile Emerson of the 1830s, is full of a sense of possibility. He has a "feeling that one is on the edge of many things: that there are many worlds from which we are separated by only a film" (SF, 147).

Believing in the inevitability of the self's growth as a condition of self-knowledge, Roethke presents himself, in the notebooks of 1943 and 1944, as a poet who is mother and child at once, finding the origins of self and the source of poetry in the fertile slime of nature. "The self must be a bridge, not a pit" (SF, 152), he says, and "the divided man becomes / Mother and child at once" (SF, 156). Mothering himself, as Whitman once did, he exclaims, "I have contempt of the self, but still indulge it like a fond mother" (SF, 156). The embryonic self becomes the condition of greatest possibility.

> My second-best shape,
> Doll, calf, or baby,
> I love you best
> In the first of morning.
> (SF, 156)

Waking to the mystery of the self, Roethke says, "A light wind keeps waking me. My handwriting grows more / crabbed and secret" (SF, 159).

In his father's greenhouse Roethke found the way to the meaning of his life and a new source for his poetry. The greenhouse was inseparable from the poet's self-discovery and new birth. "Poetry," he says, "is the discovery of the legend of one's youth" (SF, 157), and confronting these primal elements was traumatic for him. The notebooks disclose how aware he was of the poetic resources in the greenhouse and how painful and lonely this returning could be: "What was the greenhouse? It was a jungle, and it was paradise; it was order and disorder: Was it an escape? No, for it was a reality harsher than reality" (SF, 150). The "taste of self," to use Kunitz's phrase, brought him to a point of solitude where he could face the past, especially the death of his father; he refers to this solitude as "the sense of aloneness sometimes accompanied by a kind of mindless brooding, looking fixedly at sticks, old grass" (SF, 151).

This world of fragile life became the terrain of his experience as well as of something mythic, as the terrifying and procreative powers of the subhuman world in poems like "Root Cellar," "Forcing House," and "Weed Puller." Confronting such a world often took him to the edges of emotional experience: "At first a terrible depression, the sense again of impending disaster: a mixture, alternate exaltation and despair coming closer" (SF, 153). He was deeply aware of the correspondence between the primal world of the unconscious mind and the anguish of locating the origins of one's self. He speaks of feeling a "cold paralyzing horror: a glimpse into the subhuman . . . the sickness of life beginning again: the exhausting awareness of every ache" (SF, 154). As Roethke puts it: "A poem that is the shape of the psyche itself; in times of great stress, that's what I tried to write" (SF, 178).

In the largest sense, Roethke's self-discovery was infused with a spiritual craving. Every element of his growth during these years was fraught with an overwhelming sense of the Absolute. Much of his journey backward to ontogenetic and phylogenetic beginnings—to the "liquescent realm," as Kenneth Burke calls it[4]—was filled with revelation, brooding, and, at times, an ecstatic sense that could only find an adequate correspondence in his conception of God.

Roethke's notation in a notebook of 1943, "How terrible the need for God" (SF, 153), characterized his frantic quest for the Absolute and his absorption and identification with the Christian saints and mystics. In a typically boisterous manner, he exclaims: "I'd like to take every saint and personally re-fry him" (SF, 168). By 1946

4. Kenneth Burke, "The Vegetal Radicalism of Theodore Roethke," *Sewanee Review*, LXVIII (Winter, 1950), 104.

Roethke had read Evelyn Underhill's *Mysticism* more than once,[5] and in a 1942 notebook entry he lists Meister Eckhart, St. Theresa of Avila, St. John of the Cross, and St. Francis of Assisi as saints whose writings affected him most.[6]

Neal Bowers has documented a representative selection of Roethke's readings in mysticism during these years. It is probably impossible to establish a cause and effect relationship between his psychological condition (he was diagnosed as a "manic-depressive-neurotic, but not typical," "a manic-depressive psychotic, but not typical," and as a "paranoid-schizophrenic") and his mystical tendencies. And it is not my concern here to speculate on this problem. For Roethke the two seem to have been inseparable, and his new self-awareness about matters of the spirit arose in the forties from the meshing of his mental condition and his spiritual drive.[7]

Roethke's mystical proclivities did not begin with reading. The experience he had in 1935 while teaching at Michigan State reveals how closely his mental instability and his spiritual desire were linked. His first manic experience (which resulted in his being hospitalized for the first time) involved what Roethke termed at the time a mystical experience. While roaming the woods near campus one night in November, Roethke, as he later told his friend Peter de Vries, "had a mystical experience with a tree and he learned there the secret of Nijinsky." Later he told Allan Seager that during this time period "Suddenly I knew how to enter into the life of everything around me. I knew how it felt to be a tree, a blade of grass, even a rabbit."[8]

Although intuitive experience and spiritual communion with nature were not new to Roethke, the degree of intensity with which he thought about and was driven by the idea of God is a major difference between the notebooks of the thirties and those of the forties. "God robbed poets of their minds that they might be made expressions of his own" (SF, 158), Roethke says of the relationship

5. Richard Allen Blessing, *Theodore Roethke's Dynamic Vision* (Bloomington, Ind., 1974), 59.

6. Seager, *Glass House*, 161.

7. Neal Bowers, *Theodore Roethke: The Journey from I to Otherwise* (Columbia, Mo., 1982), 6, 13; Seager, *The Glass House*, 101.

8. Seager, *Glass House*, 90, 101.

between the muse and the divine. In his yearning for ultimate meaning, he began to identify with the experiences of saints and mystics. His new poetic self has something in common with mystical experience, which is "of the heart, seeking to transcend the limitations of the individual standpoint and to surrender itself to ultimate Reality. . . . By the word *heart*, of course we here mean not merely 'the seat of the affections,' . . . but rather the inmost sanctuary of personal being."[9] His spiritual need was full of self-doubt and frustration, full of a pilgrim's relentless pursuit: "Wait. Watch. Listen. Meditate. He'll come. When? No, I know He won't come. He doesn't care about me any more. No, I mean Him, the Big He, that great big three-cornered Papa. . . . A rich mystic: that's what I want to be" (SF, 168–69).

Roethke's obsessive concern with God during these years must be seen as endemic to his creative growth. The hunger for God and the desire to be a "rich mystic" was much of the force behind a poet who felt himself "on the edge of many things"—giving birth to a new self. His sense of the divine and his "terrible need for God" was a part of the creative energy that drove him. There was, for Roethke, a correspondence between the muse, the poetic act, and the reality of God. To create poetry that probed the meaning of the beauty, mystery, and terror of creation meant that the poet had to seek a knowledge of God. Carrying this correspondent notion of creation to an extreme, Roethke once wrote that "the poet is God's metaphor creating a new world from the void."[10]

Roethke's God was not a Romantic muse—a humanized holy spirit implanted within, provoked to creativity by inspiration—but, in a more orthodox sense, a God beyond the self. It was, in fact, the sheer energy of striving to encounter the presence of God that constituted much of his frantic journey. He was possessed by the sheer energy of his own discoveries during these years, and God embodied the creation's ultimate illuminating force. God became the inscrutable presence that demanded of the spiritually inclined man a ceaseless seeking and a pilgrimage that involved poetry and the birth of the self. God was ultimate experience, the terrible force that

9. Evelyn Underhill, *Mysticism* (New York, 1955), 71.
10. Rosemary Sullivan, *Theodore Roethke: The Garden Master* (Seattle, 1975), 183.

drove his poetic imagination and enabled him to discover the green-house, his personal and mythic past, and the loamy world of the mind. The realm of intuitive knowing, the world of the elemental self, and the act of transcendence were, in the end, fundamental to the nature of God that Roethke sought.

The nature of a poet's spiritual evolution is ultimately as mysterious as the nature of the human psyche. However, one aspect of Roethke's growth during this period can be seen in broader daylight. His new awareness of modern poetry and his reorientation toward poetic language had much to do with William Carlos Williams.

Roethke developed a poetic form and language that allowed him to make his journey back to the greenhouse and thus create the "journey forward," as he called it, for his persona the lost son. In liberating himself from the fixed forms and somewhat stilted and abstract language of *Open House*, he began crafting an elemental and dynamic language. This led him to the open forms of twentieth-century free verse. He began to create an organic and kinesthetic language that in *The Lost Son* embodied the nature of his mental and spiritual quest and gave shape to the idea of the psyche he wished these poems to reveal.

It is curious that no critical or scholarly attention has been paid to the influence of Williams on Roethke, though his importance to the post-World War II generation has been well documented. The beat and Black Mountain poets (Olson, Creeley, Levertov, Ginsberg, Snyder, Ferlinghetti, to name several) have discussed with elo-quence their debts to Williams, and certainly American poetry of the sixties and seventies has borne out how deeply his aesthetic has been absorbed. However, little has been said about Williams' impact on the generation that grew up after Eliot and Pound.

In his book *American Free Verse*, Walter Sutton claims that the full force of Williams' influence was "delayed by the conservative trend in the New Criticism . . . and Eliot's classicism and advocacy of the metaphysical conceit."[11] The generation upon which Williams' new poetics was lost, according to Sutton, was the "middle generation"

---

11. Walter Sutton, *American Free Verse* (New York, 1973), 152.

which included Richard Eberhart, Randall Jarrell, Robert Lowell, Howard Nemerov, Delmore Schwartz, Karl Shapiro, Richard Wilbur, and Roethke. Nevertheless, it seems clear, upon closer inspection of these poets, that Williams mattered to many of them. Eliot and the New Criticism did not prevent Lowell, Jarrell, Shapiro, and Roethke, for example, from finding Williams. At various points in their respective careers they embraced the organic and open forms and the democratic sensibility that had evolved from Whitman and found its most compelling expression in the first half of the twentieth century in the poetry of Williams. The meaning of Williams for a "middle generation" poet like Roethke tells us something significant about this crucial period of evolution in Roethke's career and revises Sutton's assertion as well.

Notwithstanding Roethke's enduring debts to American transcendentalism and British metaphysical poetry, he owed much to what he had begun to learn from modernism and the lessons of Williams, who along with Kenneth Burke was a father figure to him during the writing of *The Lost Son*. Later he would dedicate *Praise to the End!* (1951), the book which brought the entire "lost son" sequence to fruition, to Williams and Burke.

From Williams, Roethke absorbed a new sense of poetic language: a purified diction, a simpler syntax, a version of Williams' kinetic line measure, a concreteness of poetic perception and imagery, and a purer notion of "organic metaphor"—stripped of allusion and intellectual reference. Roethke found in *The Lost Son* his own American grain—a locale, the indigenous source Williams had urged American poets to discover. His true home, he now knew, was in Saginaw and the greenhouse, which, in addition to all of its mythic, religious, and psycho-sexual significance, embodied the world of his family and childhood.

It is not coincidental that Roethke's discovery of place in the Saginaw greenhouse coincided with his growing admiration for and friendship with Williams. In the early forties he learned the lessons of modernism more from Williams than from any other twentieth-century poet, and the greenhouse poems reveal his affinity with Williams' conviction that poetry is a "rediscovery of a primary impetus" inextricable from one's "local conditions," and that the poet must turn to his native ground for his material, his rhythm and poetic form. Roethke grew to understand what Williams meant when he said "nothing can grow unless it taps into the soil" and "the local is the only universal."[12] Identifying with D. H. Lawrence, Roethke claimed: "Lawrence and I are going the same way: down: A loosening into the dark, a fine spume drift" (SF, 154). And it was Lawrence who twenty years earlier had praised Williams' *In the American Grain* and exhorted American writers "to catch the spirit of her own dark aboriginal continent."[13]

In the greenhouse Roethke found form in the root, in a soil that defined past and present in a particular locale. The greenhouse was redemptive and infinitely fertile; it joined self, imagination, and psyche with the organic world in a way that Williams had expressed in "By the Road to the Contagious Hospital" some twenty years earlier:

> All along the road the reddish
> purplish, forked, upstanding, twiggy
> stuff of bushes and small trees
> with dead, brown leaves under them
> leafless vines—
>
> . . . .
>
> Now the grass, tomorrow
> the stiff curl of wildcarrot leaf
> One by one objects are defined—
> It quickens: clarity, outline of leaf
>
> But now the stark dignity of
> entrance—Still, the profound change
> has come upon them: rooted, they
> grip down and begin to awaken.

The very downward movement into the guts of the earth that is necessary for renewal and birth in Williams' poem is similar in form and content to the "profound change" that came upon Roethke as he entered the world of minimal grasses, roots, and mud. The same tough, scrupulous, crisp imagery that, in its almost botanical precision, enacts the process of the organic world in "By the Road" also characterizes Roethke's greenhouse sequence. In poems like "Cut-

12. William Carlos Williams, *Autobiography* (New York, 1951), 146, 334.
13. D. H. Lawrence, "America Listen to Your Own," *New Republic*, XXV, December 15, 1926, p. 68.

tings" and "Cuttings (later)," Roethke takes Williams' observations of nature even further, into what Stanley Kunitz has called a "near-microscopic scrutiny of the chemistry of growth."[14]

> Sticks-in-a-drowse droop over sugary loam,
> Their intricate stem-fur dries;
> But still the delicate slips keep coaxing up water;
> The small cells bulge;
> ("Cuttings")
>
> This urge, wrestle, resurrection of dry sticks,
> Cut stems struggling to put down feet,
> What saint strained so much,
> Rose on such lopped limbs to a new life?
>
> I can hear, underground, that sucking and sobbing,
> In my veins, in my bones I feel it,—
> The small waters seeping upward,
> The tight grains parting at last.
> When sprouts break out,
> Slippery as fish,
> I quail, lean to beginnings, sheath-wet.
> ("Cuttings [later]")

However concrete Roethke's imagery becomes he is able to move from detail to symbol and metaphor without ever giving up the detail. His new sense of a Williamesque world "rooted," and "grip-[ping] down" provided him with the correlative metaphors necessary to hold the intensity of his mythic concerns.

Roethke sent most of the "lost son" poems to Williams for criticism before they were published and considered Williams one of the few poets who understood what he was attempting. Williams' enthusiastic response to the greenhouse poems and to the first of the "lost son" group fueled their poetic kinship. The letters that passed between them in the forties reveal the extent to which Williams became friend, aider, and source of inspiration to Roethke. In a letter of 1944, Roethke writes:

> Dear Bill: The only reason I haven't written sooner is that I was afraid I would over-whelm you with gratitude, like a St. Bernard. In fact, I carried the letter around for a time: something to hold against the world.
>   Which sounds like self-pity, but it ain't.

14. Stanley Kunitz, *A Kind of Order, A Kind of Folly* (Boston, 1975), 100.

All those greenhouse ones and the nutty suburban ones came back from Ransom, from *Poetry*, etc. What the hell. But as an old pro, I suppose I should realize that the better you get, the more you'll get kicked in the ass. I do think the conceptual boys are too much in the saddle: anything observed or simple or sensuous or personal is suspect right now. Anything with images equals Imagism equals Old Hat. Oh well, you know all that better than I; have seen it, have been fighting it. . . . I'm particularly pleased you like *The Return* . . . it's been turned down by everybody. (SL, 111–12)

Far from being a "middle generation" poet who identified with the conservatism of Eliot and the New Critics, Roethke acknowledges how crucial Williams has been in freeing him from his earlier ways: "Dear Dr. Bill: I have been reading over your letter written to me in July 1944 and the later one about the set of short pieces I sent you. . . . It goes without saying that these letters have meant a good deal to me and have helped me, I believe, in the laborious process of getting really loosened up" (SL, 121–22). The letter of July, 1944, to which Roethke refers reveals Williams as one of the few to recognize, early on, the full-blown achievement of Roethke's new work. Spurring him on, Williams writes:

Dear Ted: These are the best things of yours that I've seen. Some of them are distinguished, you've emerged to a full and characteristic expression; they are good but they are, more important, you and with distinction as I have said. . . . Your great contribution to modern poetry may well be that you have found or are finding a way to express that generosity of spirit in a polished steel mesh or frame that can and must hold it against injury. If you can continue to make poems along that line as you have shown you can do in this batch of poems, there is no reason why you should not become one of the most distinguished poets of the day.[15]

Roethke also identified with Williams' rejection of Eliot's expatriatism; both believed that Eliot's erudition and intellectually construed mythic mode made poetry a kind of bastion of high culture that was fundamentally anti-democratic and, as Williams put it, "gave poetry back to the academics."[16]

15. William Carlos Williams to Theodore Roethke, July 14, 1944, in Theodore Roethke Collection, Suzzallo Library, Seattle, Washington.
16. Williams, *Autobiography*, 146.

But here's a long one [probably "The Lost Son"] which is the best I've done so far. It's written, as you'll see right away, for the ear and not the eye. It's written to be heard. And if you don't think it's got the accent of native American speech, your name ain't W. C. Williams, I say belligerently. In a sense, it's your poem—yours and K. Burke's. He's enthusiastic about it even in its early version. My real point, I suppose, is that I'm doing not one of these but several: with the mood or the action on the page, not talked-about, not the meditative, T. S. Eliot kind of thing. (By the way, if you have an extra copy of your last blast against T. S. E., do send it to me. I can't seem to get hold of it anywhere.) (SL, 122)

In his protestations against the conservatism of the New Critics and Eliot's academism, Roethke allied himself with Williams and his experimental temperament. Like Williams, he sought the largest meanings in the most grounded and tangible elements of the phenomenal world.

So many of Williams' outbursts in *Spring and All* apply to Roethke's new notion of poetic language in *The Lost Son:* "What I put down of value will have this value: an escape from crude symbolism, the annihilation of strained associations, complicated ritualistic forms designed to separate the work from "reality." . . . The word must be put down for itself, not as a symbol of nature but a part, cognizant of the whole—aware—civilized."[17] In the greenhouse poems, Roethke embraces the kind of organic relationship between language, external reality, and imagination that is so fundamental to Williams' aesthetic. In the early twenties, when Williams was finding his own distinctive center writing *Spring and All*, he was obsessed with the poet's need to purify the language and in doing so to return to an original condition in nature. Referring to his poetic pre-Columbian reality (America's Genesis), to which the poet must return us, Williams wrote: "To it [the imagination] now we come to dedicate our secret project: the annihilation of every human creature on the face of the earth. This is something never attempted before. None to remain; nothing but the lower vertebrates, the mollusks, insects and plants. Then at last will the world be made anew."[18] How similar is Roethke's commitment to what he

17. William Carlos Williams, *Spring and All in Imaginations*, ed. Webster Schott (New York, 1971), 102.
18. *Ibid.*, 91.

called "minimal life"; he says of the "lost son" poems: "Some of these pieces, then, begin in the mire; as if man is no more than a shape writhing from the old rock. . . . Sometimes one gets the feeling that not even the animals have been there before; but the marsh, the mire, the Void, is always there, immediate and terrifying" (PC, 40).

For Roethke, the greenhouse is the world of his birth time and a metaphor for creativity and original conditions. Like Williams, in *Spring and All*, Roethke in the greenhouse poems forces the reader to face the elemental things of creation in their fresh and vital states. Williams' muddy March landscapes in *Spring and All* resonate with certain elemental concerns and imagistic ways of reaching those concerns that remind us of Roethke in the greenhouse.

> A cold wind ruffles the waste
> among the browned weeds.
> On all sides the world rolls coldly away:
> black orchards
> darkened by the March clouds
> leaving room for thought.
> Down past the brushwood
> bristling by
> the rainsluiced wagonroad
> looms the artist figure of
> the farmer—composing
> —antagonist
> ("The farmer in deep thought")

> All that enters in another person
> all grass, all blackbirds flying
>
> all azalea trees in flower
> salt winds—
> ("Black Winds")

Although they are more botanically scrupulous and psychologically oriented than Williams' poems, poems like "Root Cellar," "Forcing House," and "Weed Puller" work through the "twiggy stuff of bushes," to use Williams' metaphor, before they get to their mythic concerns:

> Under the concrete benches,
> Hacking at black hairy roots,—

Those lewd monkey-tails hanging from drainholes,—
"Digging into the soft rubble underneath,"
Webs and weeds,
. . . .
Me down in that fetor of weeds,
Crawling on all fours,
Alive, in a slippery grave.
("Weed Puller")

Whether or not Roethke's new "lost son" poems had the ring of "native American speech," as he claimed no doubt to please Williams, he was certainly accurate in saying that they "were written to be heard," were "for the ear," and had the dynamism of "action on the page," rather than "the meditative T. S. Eliot kind of thing." He became suspicious of the "conceptual boys" and began to see the dynamic nature of poetic form and the explosive possibilities inherent in Williams' notion of meter-making poetry. As Kunitz notes, Roethke's "imagination was not conceptual, but kinesthetic, stimulated by nerve-ends and muscles, and even in its wildest flights localizing the tension when the curve is taken."[19] A passage like this from "The Lost Son" illustrates the kind of new dynamism Roethke had discovered in the early forties and the kind of dramatic activity Williams responded to so enthusiastically. Here is the lost son in the throes of mental breakdown.

Hunting along the river,
Down among the rubbish, the bug-riddled foliage,
By the muddy pond-edge, by the bog-holes,
By the shrunken lake, hunting, in the heat of summer.
The shape of a rat?
It's bigger than that.
It's less than a leg
And more than a nose,
Just under the water
It usually goes.

Such a kinesthetic imagination has something fundamentally in common with Williams' dynamic notion of form. For Williams, a poem had to grow out of the confluence of sound, imagery, and

19. Kunitz, *A Kind of Order*, 98.

diction. Much of the essence of his modernism lies in his belief that words must exist in a field of motion so that a poem can create a sense of a living process—a field of objects and things in a charged and tense syntactical relationship with one another. Williams strives to make the poem a kinetic construct set in motion by a variable measure dictated by the confluence between sound (what the ear dictates), the image, and the line's measure. What Olson has said about Williams' poetics sheds light on Roethke's changing poetic temperament, particularly in the longer "lost son" poems: "Every element in an open poem (the syllable, the line as well as the image, the sound, the sense) must be taken up as participants in the kinetic of the poem just as solidly as we are accustomed to take what we call the objects of reality; and that these elements are to be seen as creating the tensions of a poem just as totally as do those other objects create what we know as the world."[20]

Roethke found in Williams' example a poetic reality in which metaphoric fusion is total; word placement, image, and rhythm are at once aesthetic and functional. His transformation owed much to this new understanding of poetry as energized language—tense, dynamic, working from within by laws of its own. In his own ways, Roethke proclaimed Williams' aesthetics: "Don't say; create" (SF, 171); "Make the language take really desperate jumps" (SF, 171); "If he can't make words move, he has nothing" (SF, 172). Realizing that for certain poetic experiences regular meter and formal conventions impede the necessary confluence between language and meaning, Roethke began to echo what Williams had maintained for years: "There is a kind of poet who imposes unnecessary limitations and difficulties on the language; who bellows with his mouth full of butter" (SF, 173).

Williams' idea of an American grain gave Roethke the notion of his indigenous soil as a root metaphor, and his corresponding belief in poetic language, diction, and syntax that were pure and simple. Certainly *The Lost Son* is marked by a radical concreteness of language in contrast to the more metaphysically abstract language of *Open House*. As Kenneth Burke has said in his seminal essay, "The Vegetal Radicalism of Theodore Roethke," his "vocabulary of con-

20. Williams, *Autobiography*, 281.

crete things and sensible operations has enabled him to achieve a
'purified poetic idiom' . . . a purified speech that militates against
civilization's trend toward 'greater and greater abstraction from the
physical, toward a further and further separateness between men
and women, and between individual and individual.'"[21]

At the heart of Roethke's poetic liberation in the forties was the
absorption of Williams' organic notion of metaphor stripped of allu-
sion and his understanding of Williams' belief that the poem must
be "pruned to a perfect economy," with "no ideas but in things." For
Roethke, a poet who grew up on British poetry and who had learned
so much from the seventeenth-century metaphysicals, the funda-
mentals of Williams' aesthetics were a baptism into the possibilities
of twentieth-century poetry.

Time and again Roethke expressed the need to ground his meta-
phor in the specific: "I have to be concrete. Everything else scares
the hell out of me" (SF, 208); "I was a man committed to the con-
crete" (SF, 200). In rejecting the more stilted language of *Open House*,
Roethke acknowledged the subtlety of Williams' craft ("plain speech
is inaccurate but not plain words" [SF, 182]) and, recognizing what
Williams meant when he called for a "living speech,"[22] he argued
for "a speech so flexible, so plastic, we're alive to every nuance that
the language has" (SF, 196).

Roethke realized the expansive possibilities that plain speech
held for the form of a poem and the protean transformations that
could be accomplished with a return to an elemental syntax.

> Style: Break in on the reader sideways.
>   Think with the wise, talk like the common man:
>   Give a noun a full swat,
>   But adjective, not.
> (SF, 174)

To break in and to break out sideways on the reader is precisely what
Roethke's new poetic form did. He discovered that the most basic
and elemental conditions of man are most profoundly realized in a
language that is not only pure and simple but is crafted to a com-
pression that renders both internal and external worlds at once, in a

21. Burke, "Vegetal Radicalism," 80.
22. William Carlos Williams, *Selected Essays* (New York, 1948), 246.

state of perfect correspondence. He found that the short line could produce the kind of kinetic effects and high level of energy that he sought. Having learned the value of the short line from Williams, as well as from Dickinson, Blake, and Mother Goose (whom Roethke cites as his ancestors), he says: "The decasyllabic line is fine for someone who wants to meditate—or maunder. Me, I need something to jump in: hence the spins and shifts, the songs, the rants and howls. The shorter line can still serve us: it did when English was young, and when we were children" (SF, 186).

When *The Lost Son and Other Poems* appeared in 1948 it marked a new genius in American poetry and in retrospect reveals the richness and originality with which aspects of Williams' sensibility were absorbed by a poet as seemingly different as Theodore Roethke.

Given the impact Whitman would have on Roethke in the late fifties when he was at work on "The North American Sequence," the influence of Williams during this period reveals something about Roethke's place in a larger American tradition. Perhaps no poet of the twentieth century, or certainly of the modernist period, extended Whitman's American vision and idiom with the force, the innovation, and the accomplishment that Williams did. Both in a thematic and a technical sense, *The Lost Son* and "North American Sequence" are Roethke's most quintessentially American cycles. That Williams and Whitman could have exerted such influence on Roethke during his periods of change and growth reveals the degree to which he was nourished by and ultimately extended the Whitman-Williams American grain.

THREE

"The whole of life," the Greenhouse

In a grant proposal statement of 1945, Roethke referred to the green-house as "a kind of man-made Avalon, Eden, or paradise" (SL, 113). Later, in a letter to Babette Deutsche, he said, "There is the sense of motion in the greenhouse—my symbol for the whole of life, a womb, a heaven-on-earth" (SL, 141). Although in the same letter he claimed to have "read almost no psychology" and to have "worked intuitively all the time," he had, in fact, been reading much psychology, including Freud and Jung and Kenneth Burke's writings on psychology and literature.[1] No doubt his own bouts with mental illness increased his drive to discover truths about the workings of the human psyche.

During the forties Roethke developed a notion of the mind that was phylogenetic and ontogenetic, and this concept of human psychology underscored the greenhouse poems and the "lost son" sequence, giving them a blend of personal and impersonal qualities. In his quest for identity he discovered materials—the plant life of the greenhouse—which allowed him to transform a personal "I" into a representative "I." Consequently, the psychological dimensions of the greenhouse poems yield themselves to a combination of Freudian and Jungian meanings. The Freudian view of these poems that Karl Malkoff puts forth is too reductive, in this sense, because it eschews the idea of a collective psyche which was central to Roethke's concerns.

The greenhouse poems can be seen as a spiritual autobiography, for Roethke weaves together aspects of his childhood, family life,

---

1. Jay Parini, *Theodore Roethke: An American Romantic* (Amherst, Mass., 1979).

and sexuality with the progress of his soul. His achievement becomes something more than personal and so differs from the personal expressions in Lowell's *Life Studies*, Plath's *Ariel*, or Ginsberg's *Howl*. For Roethke, "nature always wears the colors of the spirit," as Emerson put it; thus, the evolution of a human spirit perceived in the process of nature becomes a way into the collective human mind.[2]

Many critics have used Romantic psychology (by Romantic I mean here Jungian rather than Freudian) to discuss the "lost son" sequence, but none has explained the greenhouse world from this perspective. Given Roethke's mythic notion of the workings of the mind, Jungian concepts are necessary in understanding the larger meanings into which the poems open. What Roethke said about the "lost son" applies also to the greenhouse: it is a "struggle out of the slime; part of a slow spiritual progress, if you will; part of an effort to be born" (SL, 140). His phylogenetic sense of his own imagination sounds Jungian and presents his notion of a collective unconscious. His sentiments about the "lost son" poems, in a letter to Selden Rodman, are also pertinent to the greenhouse poems: "It's odd: I can feel very impersonal about them, for they seem to come from a tapping of an older memory—something that dribbled out of the unconscious, as it were, the racial memory or whatever it's called. Hence, my unabashedness about them—which may be tiresome and naive" (SL, 130).

Roethke's belief that to progress spiritually it is necessary first to go back into the mind's past says a good deal about his instinctive sense of an archetypal reality. His disposition and the pull of his imagination led him to those prototypic images, forms, and experiences which constitute what Jung calls the "preconscious and unconscious" world of the psyche—the "living dispositions" of the mind which "perform and continually influence our thoughts and feelings and actions."[3] In the greenhouse poems Roethke finds ways back to some of these preconscious experiences and processes.

As a source of the beginning for Roethke, the greenhouse is also, at times, symbolic of the origins of the mind—of the unconscious.

2. Ralph Waldo Emerson, *The Selected Writings*, ed. Brooks Atkinson (New York, 1950), 7.

3. C. G. Jung, *Four Archetypes*, trans. R. F. C. Hull (Princeton, 1959), 11.

What Jung says of man's need to remain aware of the world of archetypes applies to Roethke's psychological exploration of his origins: "Man must remain conscious of the world of archetypes, because in it he is still a part of Nature and is connected with his own roots. A view of the world or a social order that cuts him off from the primordial images of life not only is no culture at all but, in increasing degree is a prison or stable."[4] In this cycle Roethke makes a version of a creation myth; the poems follow a tortuous journey in which the poet moves from darkness to light, charting the evolution of himself and the development of his consciousness. In moving from the loamy, procreant earth to the light on top of the greenhouse, Roethke moves up the evolutionary ladder. As he discovers this ground of genesis amidst the minimal life of nature, he focuses on the birth process and the sense of life as it evolves from a prelapsarian state into the painful flux of time. Because Roethke returns constantly to origins in these poems, I have found that Erich Neumann, Jung's foremost student, is also a source of concepts that continue to widen the mythic range of these poems. Neumann's idea of the Great Mother or the feminine archetype, put forth in *The Great Mother*, supplies the reader of this sequence with a metaphor that is at the center of Roethke's intentions. For here Roethke's compulsive enactments of birth rituals and his persona's inseparable relationship with the earth—which is womb, nurturer, and bearer—make the Great Mother archetype a touchstone. "Mother is mold, moddern, matter; Mutter is mud," as Norman O. Brown puts it.[5] Matter, mold, mud, and mother are all one in Roethke's seedtime. It is worth noting how deeply metaphor and autobiography were linked. At the peak of his work on the greenhouse poems when he was living in Shingle Cottage at Bennington College, Allan Seager notes, he used to pop out of his clothes and wander "around the cottage naked for a while, then dressing slowly, four or five times a day. There are some complex 'birthday-suit' meanings here, the ritual of starting clean like a baby, casting one's skin like a snake, and then donning the skin again. It was not exhibitionism. No one saw. It was all a kind of magic."[6]

4. *Ibid.*, 27.
5. Norman O. Brown, *Love's Body* (New York, 1966), 39.
6. Allan Seager, *The Glass House: The Life of Theodore Roethke* (New York, 1968), 144.

The greenhouse poems return us to a primordial time when, according to Jung and Neumann, human consciousness was undifferentiated, a time of uroboric totality when all of life's processes were, for man, united. Roethke explores in the early poems of the sequence a state of reality in which the relationship between the human psyche, nature, and the cosmos are inseparable. His sense of a mythic beginning in the greenhouse has something to do with what Neumann maintains about the origins of psychic life:

> Human life in the beginning is determined to a far higher degree by the unconscious than by consciousness; it is directed more by archetypal images than by concepts, by instincts than by voluntary decisions of the ego; and the man is more a part of his group than an individual. And similarly, his world is not a world seen by consciousness, but one experienced by the unconscious. In other words, he perceives the world not through the functions of consciousness, as an objective world presupposing the separation of subject and object, but experiences it mythologically, in archetypal images, in symbols that are a spontaneous expression of the unconscious, that help the psyche orient itself in the world.[7]

This phase of human development belongs to the feminine archetype, and in this symbolic sense the greenhouse world can be seen to embody the two basic aspects of the Great Mother. First, as the rich, fertile, loamy world of germination, the hothouse nourishes, bears, and transforms life. Neumann says, "The earth as creative aspect of the Feminine, rules over vegetative life, it holds the secret of the deeper and original form of 'consciousness and generation' upon which all animal life is based." As a "man-made Avalon," the greenhouse is also a kind of womb, an original garden containing and protecting the germinating life within it. Symbolically speaking, the greenhouse is that essential part of the feminine archetype which is "the vessel,"—the mother that "contains and protects."

Yet the greenhouse offers more than containment, protection, and nourishment. It is a world of dynamic transformation which involves the possibility of growth as well as of death and decay. Neumann says the Great Mother is good and terrible, hence her greatness. "The Great Mother embodies life and birth as well

7. Erich Neumann, *The Great Mother*, trans. Ralph Manheim (Princeton, 1955), 16.

death and destruction . . . [and] makes possible the union of positive and negative attributes." By entering "the dark space 'under' him, the underworld, the inside of the earth,"[8] Roethke explores the darker side of creation. Poems like "Root Cellar," "Forcing House," and "Weed Puller" probe a world that is not only fertile and generative but uncertain, dark, and dangerous. This far down in the earth and this far back in time (the poet's psychic time), the forces of life and death are not far apart. Neumann reminds us: "Besides the fecundated womb and the protecting cave of earth and mountain gapes [the womb of earth becomes] the dark hole of the depths, the devouring womb of the grave of death, of darkness without light, of nothingness."[9] In order to grow and to discover the meaning of his life, the poet must face this world as well. For Roethke, to be on "the edge of many things" means to confront the terrifying extremes of life; he calls the greenhouse a "hell and heaven at once, this womb of cypress and double glass" (SF, 96). If, as Neumann claims, the metaphor of the Great Mother can provide us with "the symbolic imagery of the unconscious [which] is the creative source of the human spirit in all its realization,"[10] then perhaps we can see the meaning of a poet's seed time and the progress of his childhood in several ways. In a notebook entry, Roethke wrote:

> Did I eat my mother
> Or did she eat me?
> Or was the devouring
> Done mutually?
> I cherish her image
> When I look in the glass,
> I was a true son:
> Of the middle class.
> (SF, 131)

As Kenneth Burke has pointed out, the greenhouse poems have an organic shape—"the vigor and poetic morality, of action, of form unfolding."[11] The intensity of action and interaction within and

8. *Ibid.*, 51, 41, 21.
9. *Ibid.*, 149.
10. *Ibid.*, 79.
11. Kenneth Burke, "The Vegetal Radicalism of Theodore Roethke," *Sewanee Review*, LXVIII (Winter, 1950), 79.

between the poems provides an elemental shape to an unfolding journey that is at once natural, psychic, spiritual, and poetic.

"Cuttings," the opening poem in the sequence, is Roethke's vision of an original condition. No persona intervenes; the poetic voice is not obtrusive. The struggle in the poem emanates from the natural process the poem embodies. The world of "Cuttings" is one of undifferentiated experience in which Roethke's near-microscopic perception sets the entire process of creation in motion. This is the beginning of a new rooting and a return to a time in which consciousness and perception are inextricable. The purity of nature's processes reveals the poet's struggle to be born.

> Sticks-in-a-drowse droop over sugary loam,
> Their intricate stem-fur dries;
> But still the delicate slips keep coaxing up water;
> The small cells bulge;

Here is genesis in the greenhouse. The imagery is tactile and sensuous. In the "drowse" of preconscious life, the loam is wet, "sugary," semenlike; biological growth is replete with a sexual fullness that imparts a human dimension to this experience.

The organic wholeness of the poem also proceeds, in part, from the relationship between sound and meaning. The internal half-rhymes and the assonance of the straining "i" sounds in the first stanza set in motion the precariousness of life's beginnings: "Their intricate stem-fur dries; / But still the delicate slips keep coaxing up water."

The poem shifts toward its moment of primal release:

> One nub of growth
> Nudges a sand-crumb loose,
> Pokes through a musty sheath
> Its pale tendrilous horn.

The alliterative energy of the hard, monosyllabic words generates a force that brings life forward in a painful but ultimately procreative way. Because "Cuttings" is a poem in which the poet's consciousness is inseparable from the process of the poem, both biological growth and sexual activity subsume a poetic experience; hence, the poem makes inseparable the biological, the sexual, and the poetic processes.

In the beginning, Neumann reminds us, male and female were united.[12] The meaning of origins lies in the nature of undifferentiated life. The masculine-feminine dichotomy is absent in "Cuttings." The maternal loam and those feminine receptacles, "the delicate slips," grow into the phallic "horn" which breaks ground. Even in its procreative push, the "horn" remains "tendrilous," affirming the unity of male-female properties which define a condition of original unity.

In "Cuttings (*later*)," the birth process assumes a spiritual aspect. There is a movement from the most elemental world of nudging and poking to the more mythically suggestive "urge," "wrestle," "resurrection." Rebirth is religious, sexual, and biological. Roethke's Whitmanic urge is more miraculous than the Christian resurrection: "What saint strained so much, / Rose on such lopped limbs to a new life?" Now, having effaced himself before the miracle of growth, he can identify with this experience in a deeply personal way:

> I can hear, underground, that sucking and sobbing,
> In my veins, in my bones I feel it,—
> The small waters seeping upward,
> The tight grains parting at last.
> When sprouts break out,
> Slippery as fish,
> I quail, lean to beginnings, sheath-wet.

The poet is underground in the earth womb where, sucking and sobbing, life originates. Roethke's desires assume both body and spirit. The somewhat vaginal birth rite, "tight grains parting at last," returns us to the sensual agony of the first stanza. When sprouts emerge "slippery as fish," life comes forth, sacred, as from a straining saint. In the final moment of realization, Roethke's birth is a paradoxical dying to the world. In "quailing," which means both to coagulate and curdle, in this case as a foetus at birth, and to die or succumb, Roethke suggests that the intensity of the birth experience brings us close to nonbeing. The fetal exhaustion at the moment of birth is full of a sense of awe that resonates with the numinous.

In "Root Cellar," "Forcing House," and "Weed Puller," Roethke leaves the primordial innocence of the first poems for a dark world

12. Neumann, *Great Mother*, 18.

where growth involves survival amidst mysterious and dangerous conditions. Roethke said the greenhouse was his symbol for all of life, "a heaven and hell at once." The root cellar is a rank, underground place, a world in which "diminution, rending, hacking to pieces, and annihilation, or rot and decay" are necessary for growth. Underground is a compelling metaphor for under mind— the unconscious, a place of mystery and transformation "that makes for progression of the personality and consciousness."[13] Roethke's journey into this region is a confrontation with what one must face in order to survive, grow, and affirm the self. In defining a kind of initiation experience, the poems never betray their organic wholeness; they never separate personal experience from mythical meaning. Roethke is always down on all fours, in that "slippery grave." He defined things well when he said the poet "must be willing to face up to genuine mystery. It is a dark world in which to work and the demands, other than technical, made upon the writer are savage" (PC, 42).

In "Root Cellar" we are in a fertile earth-womb, a libidinal world fraught with danger and uncertain sexual forces: "Shoots dangled and drooped, / Lolling obscenely from mildewed crates, / Hung down long yellow evil necks, like tropical snakes." Although such erotic serpentine images may echo the biblical legend of Original Sin, what seems most crucial is that what is dangerous is also procreative.

> Pulpy stems, rank, silo-rich,
> Leaf-mold, manure, lime, piled against slippery planks.
> Nothing would give up life:
> Even the dirt kept breathing a small breath.

Roethke faces the complexity and trauma of survival in the aftermath of birth. In this ambiguous world, the poet remains insistent and persistent; all life (imaginative too) struggles with its source; nothing will succumb.

Out of the rankness of the root cellar emerges a vital life. "Forcing House" is energized by a phallic exertion: "Vines tougher than wrists / And rubbery shoots, / . . . All pulse with the knocking

13. *Ibid.*, 72, 73.

pipes." Organic activity is sexual and imaginative at once: "That drip and sweat, / Sweat and drip, / Swelling the roots with steam and stench." The life that bulged in cells in "Cuttings" now swells the roots. In this damp, primal mulch, the ejaculatory roots "Shooting up lime and dung and ground bones" are part of a mythical, timeless, and collective process: "Fifty summers in motion at once, / As the live heat billows from pipes and pots." The "live heat" that "billows" asserts a release toward light, toward the spirit-force of wind.

Finally, in "Weed Puller," Roethke confronts the source of his own imaginative life, the growth of conscious and unconscious. Once again the poet finds a procreative power in seemingly opposite forces, the maw of the underworld and sexual energies. In the poem's primordial terrain, the pubic "black hairy roots" and the phallic "lewd monkey-tails" grow from the womblike "soft rubble underneath" and from those sensuous, even vaginal "fern-shapes, / Coiled green and thick, like dripping smilax." The movement toward a world of light and air in "Forcing House" ("the live heat billows from pipes and pots") points to the reality above and outside, into which the poet must grow; it suggests spirit and consciousness. *Spiritus*, which in Latin is breath or wind, or what Jung calls "original-wind-nature" represents higher consciousness. For Roethke, in a Jungian way, wind is the psychic symbol of man's spiritual life and his creative personality.[14]

In "Weed Puller," Roethke sets light against dark, the world of the unconscious against the possibility of consciousness and spirit.

> Tugging all day at perverse life:
> The indignity of it!—
> With everything blooming above me,
> Lilies, pale-pink cyclamen, roses,
> Whole fields lovely and inviolate,—
> Me down in that fetor of weeds,
> Crawling on all fours,
> Alive, in a slippery grave.

Amidst this "perverse life" he imagines the world above him pure and beautiful, yet he returns knowing he must face his own gesta-

14. Jung, *Four Archetypes*, 86–92.

tion. Still on all fours, phylogenetically linked to an earlier stage of life, the poet digs in the womb amidst the weeds of the primal slime which brings him as close to life as it does to death.

"Moss-Gathering" is a transitional poem. The intimations of a growing, conscious self in "Forcing House" and "Weed Puller" are now fully realized. The poem is characterized by a more adult dualism—a differentiated psyche that can no longer claim the world as a home or participate with complete harmony in nature's processes, as was possible in "Cuttings." Far from being only about sexual initiation, as readers and critics have so often asserted, the poem exhibits a growing degree of self-consciousness. "Moss-Gathering" marks the lost son's birth into the world and a recognition of human alienation. The dualism between human consciousness and nature is at the heart of the poem. Although the poet remembers moss gathering as a sensuous experience, his ability to see metaphorically reveals a more adult sophistication.

> To loosen with all ten fingers held wide and limber
> And lift up a patch, dark-green, the kind for
>   lining cemetery baskets,
> Thick and cushiony, like an old-fashioned doormat,

The long cataloguing lines are curtailed by a moment of recollection, "That was moss-gathering," and the poem shifts into the first moment of self-conscious memory in the sequence, marking separation between the poet's fallenness and the innocence of nature. Although there is a suggestion of sexual guilt and of masturbation, the poem centers around a larger initiation.

For the first time in the sequence, the poet is outside of the greenhouse and sees himself as a stranger, defiling the natural world rather than participating in it. There is a suggestion of rape, of violating the womb stuff from which the poet came: "But something always went out of me when I dug loose those carpets / Of green, or plunged to my elbows in the spongy yellowish moss of the marshes." Roethke descends into the primal swamp ("As if I had broken the natural order of things in that swampland") and, with an adolescent awareness, senses the meaning of his fall—the fate of human isolation and exile from Eden.

Like Ike McCaslin in *The Bear*, Roethke begins to understand the real meaning of "the natural order of things," of "some rhythm, old and of vast importance," because he emerges with a knowledge of the sin of human rapacity. His sense of feeling "mean," and of committing "against the whole scheme of life, a desecration," captures the poet's profound feeling of distress and alienation. The pun on "pulling off flesh" suggests an adolescent's guilt-ridden experience of unfulfilled sex or masturbation. The self is now separate from the wholeness of creation and aware that something is wrong.

"Big Wind" continues Roethke's journey out of the root cellar and into the world. As Roethke's symbol for life, the greenhouse is a mothering container. "Giving life, nourishment, warmth and protection,"[15] it is the womb and the poet's universe. Metaphorically, as a ship and a womb, it is a vessel in which the poet must ride into the storm. Because the greenhouse means this much to Roethke, "Big Wind" must be seen as a poem of apocalyptic proportions in which a child experiences the possibility of cosmic destruction.

The poem opens with a child's incredulity. "Where were the greenhouses going, / Lunging into the lashing / Wind?" Roethke grounds the poem accurately in the literal world of the greenhouse. Disaster is met in a pragmatic way, with the technical skill of a professional horticulturist. The reader is convinced of the factual authenticity necessary to give the poem its personal and mythical quality.

> So we drained the manure-machine
> For the steam plant,
> Pumping the stale mixture
> Into the rusty boilers,
> Watching the pressure gauge
> Waver over to red,
> As the seams hissed
> And the live steam
> Drove to the far
> End of the rose-house,
> Where the worst wind was,

The poet's ability to transform the literalness of the event into an experience of cosmic proportions gives "Big Wind" its visionary

15. Neumann, *Great Mother*, 42.

dimension. The magnitude of the storm opens the poem up into a struggle with the cosmos. The confrontation with disaster and near annihilation demands an all-night vigil in which the poet journeys into a maelstrom, facing the possibility of apocalyptic disaster: "We stayed all night, / Stuffing the holes with burlap." The personification of the greenhouse as an old woman foreshadows the old ladies of supernatural power in "Frau Bauman, Frau Schmidt, and Frau Schwartze," and the possibility of disaster is heightened by the sexual punning that implies violation and rape, as the greenhouse bucks "into the wind-waves / That broke over the whole of her."

By an act of toughness and faith, both poet and greenhouse survive. Like many of the greenhouse poems, at the center of meaning is an ability to endure trauma and continue to grow (an experience Roethke knew well from his own mental breakdowns). One must endure the "teeth" and "core" of the storm in order to emerge with some kind of faith and self-knowledge. The religious intonations of the poem's closing affirm such a faith. Like the Ark, or the Ship of Faith on the Sea of Galilee, the greenhouse, having weathered the storm, finds the light of day; it "sailed until the calm morning, / Carrying her full cargo of roses." The roses, the enduring cargo, suggest not only transcendence as Burke has noted, but also a permanence that belongs to the eternal, as in the Christian meaning of the rose. Also, one senses here the strength of the father, Roethke's father Otto, who in the next poem, "Old Florist," stands "all night watering roses, his feet blue in rubber boots,"—an act of vigilance and love.

The movement toward self-discovery culminates in "Child on Top of a Greenhouse." This seedling persona continues to look upward out of the womb, toward light and wind, spirit and knowledge. Since the greenhouse is his father's house, an ascent to the roof must be seen as a self-creative act of disobedience. Climbing on top of the greenhouse is an act of rebellious liberation from the rational, ordered world below. It marks a moment in which Roethke recognizes his identity as an artist and the precariousness that belongs to the poet's life. In a letter, Roethke recalls that "even the most foolhearty older kids wouldn't dare climb on top of the Greenhouse" (SL, 253). In the poem, the child as poet ventures to a place where only a fool would go.

A cosmic and somewhat comic pregnancy initiates this jubilant moment, with "The wind billowing out the seat of my britches." This high up the world's force has a terrific impregnating energy, "clouds all rushing eastward, / A line of elms plunging and tossing like horses." The urge for transcendence is coupled with a moment of illumination, "the streaked glass, flashing with sunlight." Transcendence demands this kind of disobedience which, regardless of its risky nature, is essential to human growth and in particular to the artist's growth. Roethke leaves the rational world and all authority down below with "everyone pointing up and shouting," and ventures toward what is for him the top of the world, where he can apprehend that "lovely and inviolate" reality he imagined in "Weed Puller."

"Frau Bauman, Frau Schmidt, and Frau Schwartze," the last poem in the sequence, was published in 1952 and added to the greenhouse sequence in *The Waking* (1953). Although some critics have argued that the poem belongs to Roethke's later sensibility and intrudes upon the sequence, it seems to me that even in its complexity it remains an organic outgrowth of the earlier greenhouse poems.[16] The adult persona oscillates between a past that is personal and mythic, and the present in which the personal and mythical past are raised to perception.

The word "Gone," with which the poem begins, evokes lost innocence and the image of the greenhouse as a part of the poet's adult memory. The three fraus, those "ancient ladies," are dominant figures in his memory and emblems of myth in his imagination. Earth mothers in the opening of the poem, they become the Fates as the poem assumes its cosmic dimension. "The Feminine is also the goddess of time, and thus of fate," Neumann reminds us. This complex relationship between time and consciousness evolves from Roethke's brilliant use of the archetype of the spinning women of Fate. According to Neumann:

> These spinstresses are originally the Great Women of Fate, the threefold form of the Great Mother, for everywhere spinning is the business of women. . . . the spinstresses are the mothers and not the daughters

16. Louis L. Martz, "A Greenhouse Eden," in Arnold Stein (ed.), *Theodore Roethke: Essays on the Poetry* (Seattle, 1965), 27.

of the sun. . . . Their presence at birth points to the knowledge born of
experience that man "comes into the world" with certain "gifts" and
"aptitudes." The reason for their appearance in threes or nines, or more
seldom in twelves, is to be sought in the threefold articulation underly-
ing all created things; but here it refers most particularly to the three
temporal stages of all growth (beginning-middle-end, birth-life-death,
past-present-future.)[17]

Evoking this threefold metaphor of the spinning women who are at
once "mothers of the sun," embodiments of life's stages, and artic-
ulators of man's birth-given gifts, Roethke remembers the green-
house. These greenhouse nursemaids possess grace and a powerful
creative energy.

> Gone the three ancient ladies
> Who creaked on the greenhouse ladders,
> Reaching up white strings
> To wind, to wind
> The sweet-pea tendrils, the smilax,
> Nasturtiums, the climbing
> Roses, to straighten
> Carnations, red
> Chrysanthemums; the stiff
> Stems, jointed like corn,
> They tied and tucked,—
> These nurses of nobody else.

They are simultaneously nurturers of life in the greenhouse and
muses who embody the poet's realization of the creative process.
Since "their presence at birth points to the knowledge born of expe-
rience that man 'comes into the world' with certain 'gifts' and 'ap-
titudes,' " they become the agents of Roethke's own poetic gift. The
intricate spinning, tying, and weaving of the strings of life is analo-
gous to the meticulous craftsmanship of the poet's art.

As the boy leaves the security of the greenhouse for the cold
world outside, the three fraus become agents of cosmic process.
Standing "astride pipes," they are, at once, full of maternal earth-
iness and supernatural force, "Their skirts billowing out wide into
tents." They assume powers of divine creation. They are radiant,

17. Neumann, *Great Mother*, 226, 228, 230.

"Their hands twinkling with wet," and mysterious and dark "Like witches." "Mothers of the sun," diviners and nurturers, they keep "creation at ease." Roethke continues to stress the deep relationship between poetic process and cosmic creation. Craftswomen and creators, the three fraus "sewed up the air with a stem; / They teased out the seed that the cold kept asleep,— / All the coils, loops, and whorls."

As the poem shifts from the mythic to the personal, and the poet identifies himself with the fragility of the greenhouse plants, Frau Bauman, Frau Schmidt, and Frau Schwartze become midwives and nurses.

> I remember how they picked me up, a spindly kid,
> Pinching and poking my thin ribs
> Till I lay in their laps, laughing,
> Weak as a whiffet;

The poem then returns full circle to the poet's present state of adult aloneness and fear, of his separation from the creative source of his past and of all life, and the tone becomes somber and elegaic as Roethke seeks to reclaim his mothers.

> Now, when I'm alone and cold in my bed,
> They still hover over me,
> These ancient leathery crones,
> With their bandannas stiffened with sweat,
> And their thorn-bitten wrists,
> And their snuff-laden breath blowing lightly over me in my first sleep.

In this moment of apotheosis, the three fraus become holy women. In the poet's cold, adult sleep—that state of separation from nature and original self—they emerge in Roethke's imagination as agents of life and givers of comfort. They affirm, as well, the force of the poet's imagination, bringing him to a realization of his gift and calling. In this second sleep of adulthood, the irrevocable movement of time can only be countered by their presence, the creative power they embody, and the mythical counterforce they pose to linear time.

When viewed in the larger context of Roethke's career, the short group of poems that comprise section 2 of *The Lost Son* are somewhat anomalous, for they are the most socially oriented poems Roethke ever published. Although they continue the poet's initiation into adult life they deal with society outside of the greenhouse. He tests the meaning of nature by venturing into the man-made world of machinery, technology, and institutional life.

"My Papa's Waltz" inaugurates the shift in the poet's journey. In the poem, Roethke reminisces and confronts his father. Beneath their comic romp he feels an odd and ambivalent closeness to his drunken papa.

> The whisky on your breath
> Could make a small boy dizzy;
> But I hung on like death:
> Such waltzing was not easy.

This love dance, a kind of blood rite between father and son, shows suppressed terror combined with awe-inspired dependency.

> The hand that held my wrist
> Was battered on one knuckle;
> At every step you missed
> My right ear scraped a buckle.

The presence of the greenhouse still lingers—"You beat time on my head / With a palm caked hard by dirt"—and old Otto, the florist, remains both a mythical and a real father. Such a duality epitomizes the fear and love, closeness and distance that seem to have defined Roethke's relationship with his father. Unlike his somewhat brittle handling of formal meter in *Open House,* here Roethke exhibits a mastery of the fixed form. Much of the poem's success grows out of the tension and irony created by the somewhat violent action of the waltz set against the steady cadence of the rhymed quatrains.

In "Pickle Belt," Roethke draws on his experience at the Heinz pickle factory where he worked the summer he was sixteen. The poem is set in motion by the contrast between his adolescent urges and the monotony of the factory, an essentially dehumanizing automated world. In opposition to the conveyor belt, an instrument inducing boredom, Roethke asserts the processes of nature, "The fruit and flesh smells mixed." The metaphoric phallus controls the poem. The phallic fruit—the pickle—is squelched by the inverted phallus—the conveyor belt. The wonderful slant and buried rhyming of "britches," "pickle," "Prickling," and "itches," reveal the poet in the throes of frustration in a world where nature's urges and mechanized efficiency are irreconcilable.

In "Dolor," the conflict between the natural and man-made worlds continues. In a sense, this white-collar office is the inversion of the greenhouse. Roethke's irony is brutal. The language of the poem has a lightness and rhythm not unlike that of the greenhouse poems, only here, of course, there is no life inside. The fullness of minimal life is inverted, and Roethke's vision is marked by an Eliotic horror of the antihuman nature of at least one element of mass society.

> I have known the inexorable sadness of pencils,
> Neat in their boxes, dolor of pad and paper-weight,
> All the misery of manilla folders and mucilage,
> Desolation in immaculate public places,
> Lonely reception room, lavatory, switchboard,

The full emotional deprivation of this world is made dramatic by Roethke's ingenious metaphors that bring together office supplies and human emotions. There is, as well, a bathos, "the unalterable pathos of basin and pitcher," that evokes the absurdity of life in the white-collar world. Essentially, "Dolor" is about death in the modern world. The inverted organicism of the office—"dust from the walls of institutions, / Finer than flour, alive, more dangerous than silica"—militates against life and, of course, against poetry and engenders the "weeds that overwhelm."

"Double Feature" continues the poet's journey into adult life. As the poet leaves the cheap entertainment in the movie theater for the "cool air of night," we are reminded of Joe Willard in *Winesburg, Ohio*. Roethke's protagonist, like Anderson's, is an adolescent artist of sorts coming to see the limitations of small town life and realizing that something greater lies out there, beyond. In a moment of poetic awareness under the night sky, the boy apprehends the cosmos— "the slow / Wheel of the stars, the Great Bear glittering colder than snow." In a moment of self-recognition he remembers "there was something else I was hoping for."

The first two sections of *The Lost Son* unfold a poet's germination time. Thematically and technically they present the materials

Roethke would use to continue forging a journey out of himself. Here he begins the song of a man's life which is at once as personal as the story of a greenhouse keeper's son and as representative as the history of a man's soul. In his deep empathy for the vulnerable and minimal life of nature, he consummates a self-effacing relationship with the world—a relationship that will come to define his knowledge of the sacredness of creation.

FOUR

The Long Poem: Praise to the End!

Roethke's own critical insights into the nature of poetry and the
workings of the imagination open the door to the fundamental ele-
ments of meaning and technique that we must understand in order
to fully appreciate the ambition and achievement of *Praise to the End!*
In "Open Letter," which appeared in John Ciardi's *Mid-Century
American Poets*, Roethke says of the sequence then still in progress,
"Each poem—there are now eight in all and there probably will be at
least one more—is complete in itself; yet each in a sense is a stage in
a kind of struggle out of the slime; part of a slow spiritual progress;
an effort to be born, and later, to become something more" (PC, 37).
Praise to the End! grew out of the first four "lost son" poems, which
took their place in the thirteen-poem sequence that made up
Roethke's 1951 collection. Although, "O, Thou Opening, O" was
written after 1951 and published in *The Waking* (1953), Roethke
thought of the poem as a belated finale to *Praise to the End!* and
always referred to it as part of the cycle. He made sure that it led off
The Waking. His careful arrangement of the poems to reveal an un-
folding journey indicates the extent to which he conceived of them
as one long work—each poem complete yet part of a stage of
growth. Unlike most of Roethke's critics, who have viewed "The
Lost Son" sequence and the "Praise to the End!" sequence sepa-
rately because they were originally published in different volumes, I
believe it essential to honor Roethke's presentation of the poems in
his third volume, *Praise to the End!* (1951), and thus to regard them as
one long work.

Although *Praise to the End!* does not have the epic-like qualities of
"Song of Myself," Whitman and Roethke strive for the same kind

of representative selfhood. *Praise to the End!* asserts the universality of a human journey so that, as Babette Deutsch has noted, the poems become "the history of a man's soul."[1] In creating the persona of the lost son, Roethke taps one of the most poignant archetypes in Western literature. For his lost son, as for those other lost sons of our literature, from Oedipus to Hamlet to Stephen Dedalus, the life journey in search of a father becomes a quest for selfhood and ultimate truth. Compelled to seek both his father Otto, the greenhouse keeper, and the spiritual Father, the lost son's journey is a kind of pilgrimage involving passage through the traumas of various stages of the life cycle: birth, separation, growth, sexual initiation, and spiritual education. In light of modern man's deracination, Roethke seeks a union between man and nature, which recalls Nietzsche's phrase "But nature which has become alienated, hostile, or subjugated, celebrates once more her reconciliation with her lost son."[2]

The structure of *Praise to the End!* is complex and paradoxical in a way that seems to distinguish it from any other long poem in American literature. Like the long poems of Whitman, Crane, and Williams—"Song of Myself," "The Bridge," and *Paterson,* for example—it has an open-ended quality and evolves organically; it grows out of itself according to the dictates of the poet's expanding consciousness, the organic accretion of metaphor, the intuitive logic of association, and the rhythmic contour of diction and rhetoric. Thus the poem has an implicit continuousness, and the implications of meaning become endlessly expansive. Although the open-ended poem finds a point of termination, it never comes to the resolution or closure which would negate the poet's underlying assumption that the self is capable of limitless growth and that the world wedded to the poet's consciousness can only exist because it can never be fully fathomed. Each discovery opens out into something unknown, something demanding confrontation and imaginative transformation. For the open-ended poet this is both self-reflexive and self-effacing.

1. Babette Deutsch, "Fusing Word with Image," New York *Herald Tribune Book Review,* July 25, 1948, p. 4.
2. Friedrich Neitzsche, *Basic Writings of Friedrich Nietzsche,* trans. Walter Kaufman (New York, 1968), 37.

Yet in contrast to the more discursive meanderings that characterize long poems like the *Cantos*, *Paterson*, or *The Maximus Poems*, a lyric tightness governs the interior movement of *Praise to the End!* It is not a long poem in projective verse or an openly enjambed poetry that moves discursively outward, often predominantly extrareferentially into a historical, literary, and social configuration. The poems are practically devoid of such allusiveness, as Roethke has proudly noted time and again in his essays.

This quality of compulsive containment makes *Praise to the End!* work differently from any other major long poem of our century. In a paradoxical way the poems open up as they move inward, and they move inward through the repeatedly obsessive returnings to certain image clusters that come to comprise the overarching metaphoric structure of the poem. The fourteen poems are endlessly spinning themselves out of a common source and giving shape to a growth that is unfolding yet simultaneously regressive. Roethke has described this quality: "Any history of the psyche (or allegorical journey) is bound to be a succession of experiences, similar yet dissimilar. There is a perpetual slipping-back, then a going-forward; but there is *some* 'progress.' Are not some experiences so powerful and so profound (I am not speaking of the merely compulsive) that they repeat themselves, thrust themselves upon us, again and again, with variation and change, each time bringing us closer to our own most particular (and thus most universal) reality?" (PC, 39). It has been said of Roethke that no other poet knew how to get lost in more ways. For him, getting lost, perpetually starting over, is the only way man can "become something more" and confront "the human problem . . . [to] find out what one really *is*: whether one exists, whether existence is possible" (PC, 20). The lost son cries, "Bless me and the maze I'm in." Norman O. Brown's notion of the maze applies perfectly to the lost son: "Meandering or labyrinthine paths, spirals, mazes . . . represent the archetypal endeavors of the divine ancestor, the prototypical man, to emerge into this world, to be born."[3]

Given Roethke's need for redoubling, for slipping backward in order to engender a necessary process of personal birth and in the larger sense a process of phylogenetic evolution, the lost son is

---

3. Norman O. Brown, *Love's Body* (New York, 1966), 38.

constantly beginning. Roethke's landscapes create a world of sources and origins: the beginning of time, the beginning of man's psychic evolution (the first shape of the mind, or as Roethke called it, "the dark pond of the unconscious"), and, of course, the beginning of the poet's personal past. He creates repeatedly his version of Genesis, when dark separated from light and the first invertebrates crawled from water and became shapes on land.

Myth and personal history are interwoven; ontogenetic and phylogenetic consciousness overlap and often merge. Nature is primal and elemental, most often inextricable from the mind's evolution and the spirit's growth. However, the poems do not exist in or create an artificial world of the psyche or a hermetic world of the unconscious. There remains embedded in the entire sequence the authenticity of personal history—the poet's childhood in his father's greenhouse. The struggle for identity must "begin from the depths . . . begin in the mire; as if man is no more than a shape writhing from the old rock" (PC, 40).

In this generating and regenerating world the lost son's imagination assumes a shape that is confluent with the organic contour of a primordial world. We return constantly to certain clusters of images and extended metaphors which create landscapes of psychological and spiritual force. The lost son is forever returning to stagnant water, rank vegetation, the minimal creatures (snails, minnows, worms, frogs), and the minute parts of flowers and plants (tendrils, cyclamen veins, small leaves). Time and again we encounter the image of the heart, which resounds with a rhetoric encompassing something biological, emotional, and religious. The house is at once greenhouse, personal past, God's house (a kind of temple), and the self.

Such obsessive imagery gives the poems an organic continuity and a cohesive interior which provide a counterforce to their sequential expansiveness. Yet one quality does not negate the other; on the contrary, the recurring metaphorical patterns working within the larger open-endedness of the poem give *Praise to the End!* a richness and complexity that lie at the very center of the lost son's drama. The poetic and technical struggle between freedom and control, open-endedness and recurring trope is simultaneously the lost son's struggle between forward motion and assertion of identity, and the necessary regressions to some form of beginning.

It might be said that this internally controlled metaphorical structure reveals how well Roethke assimilated the temperament and poetic strategies of the seventeenth-century metaphysicals—Donne, Vaughan, Herbert—from whom he learned so much as a younger poet. Given the relaxed rhythm, the loose enjambment, the colloquial diction, and the openness of form that characterize twentieth-century American free verse, Roethke's tightly organized imagery and extended metaphors have a conceitlike quality. Such internal metaphoric drama enables the lost son to return to a source within himself and in the world and, in addition, gives the poem a limit to struggle against.

Roethke's critical remarks on craft reveal his sense of tradition and point to some of the sources at work in his poems. In order to charge the poem's lyric elements with the necessary dramatic quality, Roethke deems it essential to create the tension in the poem by shifting rhythms rapidly. In "Some Remarks on Rhythm," he speaks of Donne and Herbert as poets whose dramatic diction, extended metaphors, and charged syntax create a poetic force that "can pull us up sharply" (PC, 78). Similarly, his praise of Blake's "A Poison Tree" discloses his understanding of the struggle between formal meter and free verse that comprises the complexity of rhythm in much modern poetry: "The whole poem is a masterly example of variation in rhythm, of playing against meter. It's what Blake called 'the bounding line,' the nervousness, the tension, the energy in the whole poem. And this is a clue to everything. Rhythm gives us the very psychic energy of the speaker, in one emotional situation at least" (PC, 79).

It is precisely this kind of psychic energy that Roethke is able to unleash, in part by bringing together his rhythmic sense of poets such as Blake, Vaughan, and Herbert with an American rhythm—the more sweeping, freer line, controlled by the catalog and the detailed perception, which characterizes Whitman and Williams. In the same essay Roethke remarks, "We need the catalogue in our time. We need the eye close on the object" (PC, 83). *Praise to the End!* moves continually from the nervousness of the bounding line to the cataloging rhythm of Whitman's free verse.

Roethke called these "traditional poems" whose ancestors are "German and English folk literature, particularly Mother Goose; Elizabethan and Jacobean drama, especially the songs and rants; the

Bible; Blake and Traherne" (PC, 41). Of course these are not tradi-
tional poems, but Roethke wanted to emphasize how deeply past
and present—British and American poetic traditions—are at work
in the sequence, giving the poems their structural and psychic com-
plexity and the substance and force necessary to carry out their
demands. Within these traditional elements of folk meter, extended
metaphoric organization, mystical trope, and incantatory rhythm,
the poems remain expansive, aggregately related, linked by an intu-
itive and sequential logic that makes *Praise to the End!* an incompara-
ble American poem.

However, the achievement of *Praise to the End!* is due to more than
Roethke's ability to bring these elements of poetic tradition together.
In these poems he extends certain aspects of modernism into a new
realm and in doing so becomes a major innovator of twentieth-
century poetry. If in the greenhouse the lost son found the American
grain of Williams' modernity, here he lights out for a new territory.
Eliot, Joyce, and Faulkner stand behind much of the experimenta-
tion in the poems. As Louise Bogan notes, it was "the Joyce of
Ulysses and *Finnegan's Wake* that influenced Ted in *The Lost Son*."[4]
Roethke, too, was aware of the Joycean and Faulknerian nature of
his poetic experiments. In a letter to Burke which included a draft of
"Where Knock Is Open Wide," Roethke remarks: "Hope you like
the kid's piece. Off-hand, I don't know anyone who's tried this
before, with any success. Joyce is something else. (Yeah, yeah, and a
slackened tension, often.) Also Faulkner in *As I Lay Dying* isn't the
same, and doesn't hold up so well on re-reading" (SL, 149). Not-
withstanding the defensive tone of this admission of influences (one
wonders if he had read *The Sound and the Fury*), Roethke's kinship
with Joyce and Faulkner is unmistakable.

Like Faulkner, Joyce, and Eliot, Roethke is concerned with the
relationship between poetic language, the workings of the mind,
and the shape of human consciousness. Like his modernist precur-
sors, he sought a form for language that was self-effacing and that
could dispense with the intellect's willful need to tell intrusively.

> I believe that, in this kind of poem, the poet, in order to be true to what is
> most universal in himself, should not rely on allusion; should not com-

4. Allan Seager, *The Glass House: The Life of Theodore Roethke* (New York, 1968), 149.

ment or employ many judgment words; should not meditate (or maunder). He must scorn being "mysterious" or loosely oracular, but be willing to face up to genuine mystery. His language must be compelling and immediate: *he must create an actuality* [italics mine]. He must be able to telescope image and symbol, if necessary, without relying on the obvious connectives: to speak in a kind of psychic shorthand when his protagonist is under great stress. He must be able to shift his rhythms rapidly, the "tension." He works intuitively, and the final form of his poem must be imaginatively right. If intensity has compressed the language so it seems, on early reading, obscure, this obscurity should break open suddenly for the serious reader who can hear the language: the "meaning" itself should come as a dramatic revelation, an excitement. (PC, 42)

Such a statement asserts a purely organic relationship between the creative process, the nature of poetic language, and human perception. This "psychic shorthand"—the telescoping of image and symbol to give the language a compressed intensity through which seeming obscurity becomes dramatic revelation—is not unlike what Joseph Frank refers to as the "spatial orientation" of modernist literature, in which form "is based on space-logic that demands a complete reorientation in the reader's attitude toward language . . . [and] asks its readers to suspend the process of individual reference temporarily until the entire pattern of internal references can be apprehended as a unity."[5] Yet Roethke moves beyond this kind of spatial structure into a world of "fusion, confusion, and diffusion"[6]—a world that establishes a new conjunctive relationship between consciousness, perception, poetic language, and a man's psychic history. As Roethke notes, "disassociation often precedes a new state of clarity" (PC, 41).

Like Joyce in *A Portrait of the Artist as a Young Man* and Faulkner in *The Sound and the Fury*, Roethke creates a world in which perception is undifferentiated; "We think by feeling. What is there to know?" he would say later in "The Waking." Emotional, sensory, and intellectual knowledge are inseparable from one another and from rhythm, sound, and image. To Faulkner's Benjy, "Caddy smells like trees,"

5. Joseph Frank, *The Widening Gyre* (New Brunswick, N.J., 1963), 13.
6. Kenneth Burke, "The Vegetal Radicalism of Theodore Roethke," *Sewanee Review* LXVIII (Winter, 1950), 103.

and for Joyce's Dedalus, "the moo cow" inaugurates the process of knowing. In the consciousness of both characters, words, sound, rhythm, and reality are intertwined. Similarly, the lost son experiences a reintegration of human processes—a liberation from the limits of the intellect, from, say, Prufrock's cerebral speculation, and also from the tyranny of any single sense. The lost son lives in a world where all sensory experiences interpenetrate. Because Roethke engages in a dialogue with everything and anything, language creates a sense of polymorphous perversity; experience is often erotic and mystical at once.

Creating a language of innocence is a way into the child's mind. In the Christian-Romantic tradition the child, for Roethke, is symbolic of unified being and an original relation to the universe. The child possesses a purity of faith, a quality of ultimate receptivity and an uncorrupt self. Christ's admonition that to enter the kingdom of heaven we must "become like children" underscores Roethke's sentiment. For Roethke believes in this inherent illuminative capacity of the child's being. The lost son affirms that when we are closest to the essence of things we are closest to the divine. And in his variation on Wordsworth, the lost son is father to the man.

However, Roethke expands this notion of the child's divine knowledge into Whitman's world where the animals—nonhuman innocence—possess a quality of sacred being and an implicit knowledge of life's holiness. Whitman says, "I think I could turn and live with animals, they are so placid and self-contained, / . . . They bring me tokens of myself, they evince them plainly in their possession." Roethke extends this relationship between man, innocent life, and the divine to include the most shapeless substances of life—the dumb forms of the subhuman and the minimal life. The lost son cries, "Blessed be torpor. / Not all animals / Move about."

The inclusive nature of the lost son's being allows him to have a vital and dynamic contact with the world. The barely recognizable elements of organic life are part and parcel of himself and of something divine.

> If the dead can come to our aid in a quest for identity, so can the living—
> and I mean *all* living things, including the sub-human. This is not so
> much a naive as a primitive attitude: animistic, maybe. Why not? Every-
> thing that lives is holy: I call upon these holy forms of life. . . . For there *is*

a God. . . . He moves and has His being. Nobody has killed off the snails. Is this a new thought? Hardly. But it needs some practicing in Western society. Could Reinhold Niebuhr love a worm? I doubt it. But I— we—can. (PC, 24, 27)

This world has not only a subject/object abridgment but a radical, paratactical vision that defines such a universe; an organic parity exists among all things. For Roethke this is not a philosophical generality or a simple act of literary personification, but an inclusive notion of consciousness that finds psychic, emotional, and sensory equivalents in all aspects of the natural world. Reinforcing Roethke's comments, Delmore Schwartz notes an inclusiveness to Roethke's sensibility that involves the very movements of life itself when he describes Roethke's imagination in light of "Valery's remark that the nervous system is the greatest of all poems."[7]

Roethke's world contains something more dynamic—something simultaneously psychological, biological, and spiritual—in comparison with a more traditional pantheism or even Emerson's somewhat depersonalized and general nature mysticism. Emerson speaks *about* nature, often theorizing from a distance. Although he calls for "an occult relation between man and the vegetable" (something Roethke obviously takes to heart) and discusses nature as the symbol of the spirit, he remains somewhat aloof from the organic stuff of life. Nature remains Ideal, and even Emerson's most emotional experiences with it seem to be experiences of the mind which involve a more abstractly metaphysical notion of reality. As Emerson says, "the world is emblematic . . . the whole of nature is a metaphor of the human mind."[8]

In light of this, Roethke's vegetal world reveals a deeply intimate relationship between the particulars of nature (tendrils, moss, weeds, orchids, mildews, scums, snails, otters, frogs) and the conditions of the body, mind, and spirit. Roethke establishes more than a Buberian dialogue with nature; he engages it often with a primary nakedness and is effaced through a humility which enables him to treat the things of the world on their own ground. He is able to

7. Delmore Schwartz, *Selected Essays*, eds. Donald A. Dike and David H. Zucker (Chicago, 1970), 187.
8. Ralph Waldo Emerson, *The Selected Writings*, ed. Brooks Atkinson (New York, 1950), 18.

surrender himself to organic life and yet transform it in order to find the properties and processes within it that make man whole. This paradox, of course, requires immense struggle, a struggle in which Roethke as man and poetic persona is constantly involved. Roethke knew and loved nature too well to exploit it poetically for the self's egotistical need or for an exclusively literary end. He needed to find that point of conjunction and fusion at which the fullest part of the self and the most organically complete elements of nature could meet, neither compromising the other's integrity. In "The Long Alley," the lost son says: "Reach me rose, sweet one, still moist in the loam, / Come, come out of the shade, the cool ways, / The long alleys of string and stem."

In rearranging the order of the poems, Roethke began with "Where Knock Is Open Wide," the poem that inaugurates the lost son's birth of consciousness. The title derives from Christopher Smart's lines in "Song to David"—"Where ask is have, where seek is find, where knock is open-wide"—which suggest that the process of journeying forth is inseparable from the creation of selfhood, from becoming, as Roethke put it, "something more." Both Smart's lines and Roethke's title echo Jesus, who reminds us that with innocence and courage one need only "knock and it will be opened."

In his first phase of infantile knowing, the child's consciousness moves in a variety of associational ways, with a constant internal dynamic relating sound, play, rhythm, and imagery.

> A kitten can
> Bite with his feet;
> Papa and Mamma
> Have more teeth.
>
> Sit and play
> Under the rocker
> Until the cows
> All have puppies.

Because the child's knowledge is undifferentiated, more sentiently complete, there is an appropriate confusion of sensory experience. A kitten's scratch is associated with the act of biting, the fear of pain with the child's need for security and protection. Hence, the shift to

"Papa and Mamma" who provide protection and "Have more teeth."

One might say that Roethke's lost son emerges out of "the Ninth-month midnight" into a world before the Fall, a prelapsarian world in which the son's literal father and God the Father are inseparable. In this eternity, the son's "ears haven't time." Such cyclical time is marked by an undifferentiated relationship with the world. Seeing, feeling, and being are joined—they define one another. In a Words-worthian sense, the child is father to the man, and if in Roethke's world we don't come into the world "trailing clouds of glory," we emerge from other eternal sources—"seed," "fish," "water"—all of which encompass the immortal past: "What's the time, papa-seed? / Everything has been twice. / My father is a fish." In this mythical time when "everything has been twice," father and fish are united—biologically and spiritually the source of life.

Personal experience is inseparable from a nonlinear orientation in this phase of psychic development. Although he knows his uncle has died ("My uncle's away, / He's gone for always, / I don't care either."), he does not understand mortality. This procreative seeing persists, "I know her noise. / Her neck has kittens," and he affirms his carefree innocence: "I sang I sang all day."

The child's awareness of the dark is the first step toward an independent identity and the inevitability of aloneness and separa-tion. With his animistic mode of association the lost son imparts the coming of the dark to the owl: "I know it's an owl. He's making it darker." The warmth of the womb is slowly diminishing, and only "Some stones are still warm." As the dark brings confusion, the child senses the existence of time, of some form of eschatology ("Who keeps me last?"), and calls out to his father: "Fish me out. / Please." In the naive grammatical gymnastics of the child's mind, "Fish" is both verb and noun, heavenly and earthly father, and when he asks for God, "God, give me a near," the transforma-tion of the preposition "near" into a noun not only abridges the child's spatial orientation, but with its pun on "ear" also makes his pleas more poignant. In his primary, synesthetic way of knowing, the child associates flowers with his father ("I hear flowers."); fa-ther, florist, creator of life are all brought together. This is what Roethke means when he speaks of an intimate and primary knowledge of reality that could be created by telescoping "image and symbol . . . without relying on the obvious connectives" (PC, 42).

Reverting to the "liquescent realm," as Burke calls it, the child recalls fishing with his father. Everything is, as Roethke says, "compelling and immediate," with rapidly shifting rhythms: "We went by the river. / Water birds went ching. Went ching." Mythic and personal experience are united, for the literal experience is also the spirit's quest. The child cries out, "I was sad for a fish," and seeking the father identifies with the fish: "Don't hit him on the boat, I said, / Look at him puff. He's trying to talk. / Papa threw him back."

The child's experience of his father's death marks his fall from innocence. The fusion and at times confusion of earthly father with heavenly Father reveals the magnitude of trauma the lost son experiences.

> He watered the roses.
> His thumb had a rainbow.
> The stems said, Thank you.
> Dark came early.

"Rainbow" and "roses" suggest the father's heavenly or paradisical omnipotence. He had more than a green thumb; he brought forth all life.

Roethke's persona now becomes the lost son. He can no longer sing, in the face of death, "I don't care either." When the child cries out "I fell! I fell!" he recognizes that a fatherless world must be confronted. What was once warm, infinite, and timeless is now threatening, cold, harsh, and incomprehensible: "Nowhere is out. I saw the cold. / Went to visit the wind. Where the birds die." In accepting the loss of Papa who had "more teeth," the son must affirm an identity of his own, in order to protect himself: "I'll be a bite," and like a fish, a bite on his father's line as well, waiting.

The process of becoming, or forging an identity, begins in the wake of grief and in separation from the father. Otto, the father-florist, and God remain inseparable. Now in exile from the kingdom—from the greenhouse and the eternal time of the father's protection—the child enters a new phase. "I'm somebody else now. / . . . Have I come to always? Not yet." Everything is in abeyance and flux as the lost son journeys forth alone: "Maybe God has a house. / But not here."

The next two poems "I Need, I Need" and "Bring the Day!" commence the lost son's journey into time, into time after the Fall. In Roethke's words, "The protagonist, a little boy, is very sad" (PC, 75). The language is still that of the child, but the nursery rhyme jump-rope songs and the innocent word play are underscored by a sense of loss, separation, and exile. Feeling separate from his mother as well, the child tastes his own aloneness. "A deep dish. Lumps in it. / I can't taste my mother." In this time of painful new beginnings he can only say, "Mamma, she's a sad fat."

A sense of insomnia and restlessness characterizes much of the boy's dreamlike estrangements.

> A sneeze can't sleep.
> Diddle we care
> Couldly.
>
> Went down cellar,
> Talked to a faucet;
> The drippy water
> Had nothing to say.

Distancing himself from death, he still defines survival and self by what bites: "Do the dead bite?"

The child's growing self-knowledge is embedded in the jump-rope nursery rhymes of section 2. Roethke was greatly attracted to what he called the "memorable speech" of Mother Goose's language. He felt a kinship with the oral tradition in English poetry and he found in the nursery rhyme some of the most natural and powerful elements in our language. Nursery language suited his ear as well as his dramatic notion of lyric poetry. "Rhythmically, it's the spring and rush of the child I'm after—and Gammer Gurton's concision: *mutterkin's* wisdom" (PC, 41). He discovered that the "incantatory effects" and "strongly stressed swat rhythms" of nursery poetry involve the reader in a dynamic way. In accord with Whitman's claim that reading poetry must involve a "gymnast's struggle" in which "the reader must do something for himself,"[9] Roethke finds that "the hortatory" of the nursery rhyme "often makes for the memorable. We're caught up, involved. It is implied we do something" (PC, 77).

9. Walt Whitman, *Leaves of Grass and Selected Prose*, ed. Scully Bradley (San Francisco, 1949), 545.

An implicit irony lurks in the seemingly naive nursery speech, for beneath the playful rhythms and catchy repetitions is an undercurrent of trauma—hostility, fear, and sexual frustration. The child's world is diminished; it is without gratification ("Even steven all is less") and without sweetness or pleasure ("I haven't time for sugar."). It is even comically grotesque: "Put your finger in your face, / And there will be a booger."

He rejects the uncompromising faith in absolutes that ordered the world before the Fall; "The Trouble is with No and Yes / As you can see I guess I guess." Since a "hat is a house, / I hid in his," the child still measures life by what encloses and protects him, or what once did. Now, alone and vulnerable, his need for security and power is great: "I wish I had ten thousand hats, / And made a lot of money."

The struggle with grief remains essential to the child's attempt to find an identity. "Not you I need," he replies to the lost self. And as birds continue to be associated with some unapproachable place where the dead go, the lost son exclaims, "Stop the larks, Can I have my heart back?" The movement toward self-affirmation in the final section is charged with a phallic humor and sexual force that recall the procreative power of his father and further the boy's identity. "When you plant, spit in the pot. / A pick likes to hit ice. / . . . My hoe eats like a goat."

The title "Bring the Day!" celebrates the coming of the light. The sexual energy of "I Need, I Need" continues in nature's procreative activity, with even a preadolescent suggestion of "the birds and the bees."

> Bees and lilies there were,
> Bees and lilies there were,
> Either to other,—
> Which would you rather?
> Bees and lilies were there.

The child's naive struggle with final ends ("Who keeps me last?," "Have I come to always?") has given way to a new sense of immanence in which time, sexual growth, and the spirit's movement exist in nature. Roethke inverts the sterility of Eliot's spiritual dryness in *The Waste Land*, where the absence of water and rock becomes a tormenting reality: "If there were the sound of water only / Not the cicada / And dry grass singing / But the sound of water over rock." Conversely, the lost son cries:

> I've listened into the least waves.
> The grass says what the wind says:
> Begin with the rock;
> End with water.

Even though after the fall the poet cannot return to a prelapsarian innocence, "I can't marry the dirt," he knows that to create an independent identity he must move forward and reintegrate himself with nature. In the light of day, after the night of grief ("The chill's gone from the moon. / Only the woods are alive."), the lost son is startled into a new intimacy between his inner world and the rhythms of nature and knows "Everything's closer." Nature becomes animated with the boy's sexual urgings and a growing phallic strength, "When I stand, I'm almost a tree."

> The green grasses,—would they?
> The green grasses?—
> She asked her skin
> To let me in:
> The far leaves were for it.

In "Bring the Day!," "Hardly any old angels are around anymore," because the lost son has joined the world of experience. Realizing that the trouble is with "No and Yes," and unlike Blake's child of experience in "The Sick Rose," the lost son says, "The worm and the rose / Both love / Rain." Since he has confronted and accepted mortality, the boy can say, "The dust, the long dust, stays," and a new journey toward grace can begin. In a miraculous way that evokes Jonathan Edwards' sailing spiders in "Of Insects," Roethke's child affirms a new beginning in which nature propels the poet into the fullest time of year: "The spiders sail into summer. / It's time to begin! / To begin!"

Thus, "Give Way, Ye Gates" marks a transition in the sequence. The "time to begin" calls for great release, as the title suggests, to break through the inhibitions of the ego, to break down the walls that separate the spirit, body, and imagination from the world. In "Give Way, Ye Gates" and the two poems that follow it, "Sensibility!

O La!" and "O Lull Me, Lull Me," a more excited surge forward and a more vehement assertion of self characterize the lost son's awakening. Sexual growth and the spirit's movement are wedded to the rhythms of nature.

The suffering in the opening of "Give Way, Ye Gates" is submerged in nature: "Believe me, knot of gristle, I bleed like a tree." Punning in a typical Roethkean fashion, the lost son exclaims, "I could love a duck." Everything is full of a seductive desire in the somewhat bawdy Elizabethan mode.

> Such music in a skin!
> A bird sings in the bush of your bones.
> Tufty, the water's loose.
> Bring me a finger. This dirt's lonesome for grass.

The conjugal relationship between poet and nature makes this a kind of love poem in which the boy's lover is embedded in the world. Full of his phallic self and the heat of sexual desire, the lost son confesses, "I've let my nose out; / I could melt down a stone."

This landscape of growth and self-assertion becomes increasingly elemental—"I've played with the fishes / Among the unwrinkling ferns"—a meandering backward through primal territory. Such sliding back to an original slime is for Roethke a necessary condition of growth. As in "Cuttings," and "Cuttings (later)" this is a world of first arousal: "Touch and arouse. Suck and sob. Curse and mourn." There is a correspondence between this primordial condition in nature and the origins of the mind and of mankind evolving out of the world. We enter a world of the unformed, of shapes and vague movements, of shadows and sounds. Everything is elemental and suggestive:

> It's a cold scrape in a low place.
> The dead crow dries on a pole,
> Shapes in the shade
> Watch.

A mood of eeriness is created, in part, by the interior rhyming, assonance, and alliteration of "scrape" and "place," "crow" and "pole," "shapes" and "shade." The image of the crow on the pole recalls Roethke's earlier poem "Night Crow," in which he sees in a landscape of crow and tree the origins of the mind. Now the lost son, with a cumulative sense of man's development, hears "the clap of an old wind." His "heart's original knock" defines a continuity of life which unites the lowest forms of cold-blooded invertebrates with man; mind and water are one. Thus, from the "high-noon of thighs," the poet regresses to the watery beginnings where the mind's "deep stream remembers: / Once I was a pond." This is both the primordial water out of which life first crawled and the deep water of the interior, Roethke's favorite metaphor for the unconscious mind: "What slides away / Provides."

There is in "Sensibility! O La!" a more poetically self-aware exploration of the archetypal landscape created in "Give Way, Ye Gates." The lost son continues to wander in that subhuman world where the awakening of all forms of life is an awakening of spirit and imagination; everything resonates with a sense of cumulative identity: "I'm the serpent of somebody else." Roethke called the unconscious a "dark pond," and here where the world is full of feminine properties and sexual undertones, the lost son exclaims: "See! She's sleeping like a lake: / Glory to seize, I say." Out of formless substance and darkness the lost son finds the origin of the human psyche as well as the most universal form of identity. He is linked with all life— organic and inorganic—and thus is able to make the world a home in the most inclusive way: "In the fair night of some dim brain, / Thou wert marmorean-born."

The search to find form, to make a substance out of amorphous beginnings, involves for the lost son, who is forging an artistic identity as well, the tapping of the mind's imaginative source and original power. Hearing the sound of first things, "The lake washes its stones," he hears the mind's primal warblings. The poet can only confront himself as he proclaimed necessary in "Open House," with "nakedness my shield." Thus "naked and entire," he embraces the journey ahead, the repeated need for beginnings—"It's a long way to somewhere else." Light and dark continue to define the struggle of the self that seeks definition and poetic power. When Roethke follows his assertion, "I have," with the onomatopoetic, "La, la," he confirms the sound of the voice, the music of verbal sound, with his own existence, his life taking shape. Unafraid to journey into the mystery of dream and the unconscious, he asks, "Has the dark a door?" And he answers as the poet whose growing self-realization can only come from a slow accretion of form. The poet's identity with all matter ("marmorean-born") enables him to go a step beyond the "time to begin" and proclaim an existence for which he has struggled. "I insist! / I am."

In his insistence upon identity the lost son finds a world in which the divine and the organic are inseparable. In "O Lull Me, Lull Me," Roethke ingeniously employs religious and even ecclesiastical metaphors to render sacred the simple act of breathing: "One sigh stretches heaven. / In this, the diocese of mice, / Who's bishop of breathing?" What Roethke would later call a "first heaven of knowing" underscores the lost son's expanding sense of grace, his constant, growing compassion for the weak and the dumb. Roethke, like Whitman ("the tree-toad is a chef-d'oeuvre for the highest"), finds in the meek and insignificant the presence of God and the spirit's life. This Christianlike notion that the meek shall inherit the earth carries a strong sense of identification and empathy with the humble and helpless. Such consciousness enables the lost son to find a home in the world and to affirm a radical unity between the self and, in the most expansive sense, the substance of life; everything in Roethke's world is still close to the source of creation.

"The air, the air provides. / Light fattens the rock." Having moved from a time to begin in "I Need, I Need," to what provides in "Give Way, Ye Gates," to the insistent self of "Sensibility! O La!," the lost son can begin to apprehend the "Way to another grace" and can feel his spirit alive in the world: "I see my heart in the seed." In an almost frenzied, mystical way he surrenders his identity to the persistent creatures, "crazed and graceless, / A winter-leaping frog."

The poem builds to a series of ecstatic, Blake-like affirmations.

> I'm more than when I was born;
> I could say hello to things;
> I could talk to a snail;
> I see what sings!
> What sings!

Such ecstatic joy is the result of being able to have an intimate dialogue with the *Other* in nature. The poet's voice expands outward, becoming part of a larger rhythm in order to create a music out of the world.

"The Lost Son" inaugurates a shift in time and growth in the sequence, with rhetoric and diction that are less naive and childlike. The poem is anchored in personal memory and adheres more closely to the historical event of Roethke's father's death, which occurred when the poet was thirteen. We know from "On the Road to Woodlawn" that Woodlawn is the cemetery where the poet as a boy would help his father deliver flowers to funerals as well as being the site of the father's burial.

The coffin's closing lulls the lost son out of personal memory into a journey through a homeless world: "At Woodlawn I heard the dead cry: / I was lulled by the slamming of iron." This is not a child's mythical fall from innocence into an acceptance of mortality as in "Where Knock Is Open Wide," but an adolescent son's search for his father. Here the regressive journey does not involve the kind of playful incredulity that marks the child's growing awareness in "Where Knock Is Open Wide." This original slime holds little fecundity; the world is cold, wet, and dark: "A slow drip over stones, / Toads brooding wells." What Jacob Boehme says of the relationship between birth and death is true of the lost son's anguish: "Fierce wrathful death is thus a root of life . . . for out of death is the free life born. . . . But the will to anguish, which gives birth to the anguishful nature, and which is called Father, *that* is impossible to search out. . . . For the angelic light-world, and also this our visible world, must have the essence of dark death for their life and source; there is continual hunger after it."[10]

No longer fishing with his father as in "Where Knock Is Open Wide," the lost son is alone over stagnant water that conjures up the sterility of Eliot's Fisher King.

> Fished in an old wound,
> The soft pond of repose;
> Nothing nibbled my line,
> Not even the minnows came.

The "old wound" is the self's personal pain as well as a kind of *weltschmerz* that even suggests Christ's stigmata. Now the lost son's world is symbolized by "an empty house"—that emblem of the son's devastated self and the greenhouse abandoned by his father.

10. Jacob Boehme, *Six Theosophic Points and Other Writings*, trans. John Rolleston Earle (Ann Arbor, Mich., 1958), 72.

> Sat in an empty house
> Watching shadows crawl,
> Scratching.
> There was one fly.

Roethke's image plays off of the grotesque, secular fly of Dickinson's "I heard a fly buzz." For Dickinson the dramatic anticipation of seeing the light—the long-awaited moment of entrance into the kingdom—is abruptly short-circuited by an interposing fly who causes a blackout, reduces the world to darkness, and leaves the poet a failed seer and a lost pilgrim. Furthering such irony, in Roethke's house all anticipation is inverted. We move from emptiness to nothingness, from the comically grotesque act of "Scratching" to the banality of the fact that "There was one fly."

The rhetoric of questioning and the abruptly shifting rhythms of the interior dialogue create a frantic movement and a desperate search: "Tell me: / Which is the way I take." There is a continued movement downward, from an airy expanse, "the pasture of flat stones" and "sheep strewn on a field," to a world of rank vegetation.

> Hunting along the river,
> Down among the rubbish, the bug-riddled foliage,
> By the muddy pond-edge, by the bog-holes,
> By the shrunken lake, hunting, in the heat of summer.

In the "Lost Son" sequence, this stagnant water of marsh and swamp is a central and symbolic landscape, the landscape of the psyche "under great stress." In the bog, death and life are undifferentiated. The poet's hunt—his search for his father and for himself—involves extreme grief and pain. What has been previously suggestive of the primordial, archetypal, and fecundating source is inverted to invoke things rank, oppressive, wasted. The lost son is forced inward to his shrunken self. What was once the fertile pond of psyche and imagination, "rocking with small fish," is now a kind of sewage. Roethke's lost son is much like Hamlet, who sees his world as "an unweeded garden / That grows to seed; things rank and gross in nature / Possess it merely."

Roethke's use of the riddle creates a continuous sense of urgency; it is as if the lost son must pass a certain test of initiation in order to survive. The fish riddles move him toward life once more: "It's less than a leg / And more than a nose, / Just under the water / It usually goes." There remains the constant need to evolve from the beginning—from the fish in water—from the mystery and origin of life. In section 2, "The Pit," Roethke employs a technique similar to the riddle, attaching an urgency to the lost son's need to grapple with such truth. His rhetoric has an oracular, sphinxlike quality, an opaque, elusive way of questioning and answering (each answer reveals some truth while pointing the way to something unfathomable) which is a confrontation with Truth. As Mary and Herbert Knapp have noted in their book on children's folklore, "solving traditional riddles is a matter of life and death," for all riddles have something imperative about them.[11] Certainly the lost son, in his quest to forge an identity, must like Job or Oedipus face the ultimate questions in the opaque form of a riddle. As Job confronts with awe and trembling the unfathomable nature of creation, and in doing so must literally confront God, so too does the lost son face first principles.

> Where do the roots go?
> Look down under the leaves.
> Who put the moss there?
> These stones have been here too long.
> Who stunned the dirt into noise?
> Ask the mole, he knows.
> I feel the slime of a wet nest.
> Beware Mother Mildew.
> Nibble again, fish nerves.

In section 3, "The Gibber," nothing provides, and there is an extreme sense of alienation and estrangement from the world. As with Hamlet, everything within the self and in the world is out of joint, hostile and terrifying: "Dogs of the groin / Barked and howled." The son is orphaned by father and mother (symbolically sun and moon): "The sun was against me, / The moon would not have me." A hellish vegetation subsumes his suicidal desire.

> The weeds whined,
> The snakes cried,

---

11. Mary Knapp and Herbert Knapp, *One Potato, Two Potato* (New York, 1976), 104.

> The cows and briars
> Said to me: Die.

Orphaned and on this thin edge between being and nonbeing, the lost son falls into a feverish, cold sweat: "I'm cold. I'm cold all over. Rub me in father and mother. / Fear was my father, Father Fear." Everything happens in an atmosphere of hallucination and ghoulishness.

> What gliding shape
> Beckoning through halls,
> Stood poised on the stair,
> Fell dreamily down?

Finally it is the poet's tongue and mouth (the organs of speech and poetic utterance) that awaken him, and the long-lined stanza that follows is a burst of psychic energy which restores the lost son: "All the windows are burning! What's left of my life? / I want the old rage, the lash of primordial milk!"

The way back from near death is of course through the greenhouse. Section 4, "The Return," is a recollection. Still searching for his father, the lost son remembers a night he spent as a boy in the "long greenhouse"—which becomes the symbol of this night journey. In his all-night vigil, certain life signs keep him awake and alive: "The roses kept breathing in the dark. / . . . There was always a single light / Swinging by the fire-pit." The coming of the father in the morning is cathartic and even ecstatic. The "Pipe-knock," as Roethke has explained, is both the steam pipes knocking and his father knocking his smoking pipe against the steam pipes. The father is benevolent and life-giving as well as awe-inspiring and full of a numinous character. Roethke never forgot his father's Prussian sense of order and discipline; when he comes there is a "Scurry of warm over small plants." The boy cries, echoing his father, "Ordnung! Ordnung!," a German expression meaning that everything is in its proper place, all is right with the world. Of this moment Roethke says, "the papa on earth and heaven are blended" (PC, 39). Everything now turns toward the light.

Echoing Eliot's in-between season in "Little Gidding," Roethke's last section, " 'It was beginning winter,' " brings together the irrational force of the unconscious which dominates the first three sections of the poem with the order and stasis achieved in the green-house section. The landscape is transformed from the physical to the metaphysical, and the movement is from a visionary kind of seeing, in which dead nature becomes alive, beautiful, and il-luminative, to a contemplative, meditative, and finally metaphys-ical reality, in which the poet seeks to know by mind as well as by emotion.

> It was beginning winter,
> An in-between time,
> The landscape still partly brown:
> The bones of weeds kept swinging in the wind,
> Above the blue snow.
>
> It was beginning winter,
> The light moved slowly over the frozen field,
> Over the dry seed-crowns,
> The beautiful surviving bones
> Swinging in the wind.
>
> Light traveled over the wide field;
> Stayed.
> The weeds stopped swinging.
> The mind moved, not alone,
> Through the clear air, in the silence.

The immanence of the divine is rendered through paradox: "Still-ness becoming alive, / Yet still?," "Light," and "light within," and "light within light" involve a union that exists between the poet's inner spirit, nature, and the divine. A kind of patience and humility confirm the lost son's struggle toward understanding.

> A lively understandable spirit
> Once entertained you.
> It will come again.
> Be still.
> Wait.

This final moment of understanding and ordering experience is more intellectual. The mind contemplating and comprehending as-sures the lost son of the value of his struggle toward affirmation and knowledge.

"The Long Alley," "A Field of Light," and "The Shape of the Fire" grow out of the contour of light and dark that governs "The Lost Son." Because for Roethke every stage of growth demands a reversion to a primal condition in nature and involves the tapping of a source that is phylogenetic as well as ontogenetic, all these poems begin in a marsh, a swamplike primordial world of vegetation and water, a world in which life and death, stagnancy and fertility are inseparable. This is, as Erich Neumann points out, the vegetative world that engenders the animal world. "The Long Alley" opens as "A river glides out of the grass. A river or a serpent. / A fish floats belly upward." In "A Field of Light," the stagnant, primordial waters give birth to the lost son's first shape of mind.

> Came to lakes; came to dead water,
> Ponds with moss and leaves floating,
>
> . . . .
>
> I was there alone
> In a watery drowse.

For Roethke this primordial landscape continues to be the original form of the mind and of poetic consciousness.

> The ear hears only in low places.
> Remember an old sound.
> Remember
> Water.
> ("The Long Alley")

The struggle for just one sound is the beginning of life; "The softest cove / Cried for sound." As Kunitz says, "The subhuman is given tongue; and what the tongue proclaims is the agony of coming alive, the painful miracle of existence."[12] In "The Shape of the Fire" water "thus recedes to the crying of spiders" and "A cracked pod calls." The origins of life always contain some process of poetic utterance. "A low mouth laps water. Weeds, weeds, how I love you," exclaims the lost son.

Here the son's religious search intensifies, the quest for God and illumination becoming more self-conscious. "There's no filth on a plateau of cinders. / This smoke's from the glory of God," the poet asserts in "The Long Alley." Once again the greenhouse is the site of

12. Stanley Kunitz, "News of the Root," *Poetry,* LXXII (January, 1949), 25.

some crucial experience. Seeking illumination, the lost son identi-
fies with and yearns for a union with the struggling, sprouting life.

> Come littlest, come tenderest,
> Come whispering over the small waters,
> Reach me rose, sweet one, still moist in the loam,
> Come, come out of the shade, the cool ways,
> The long alleys of string and stem;
> Bend down, small breathers, creepers and winders;
> Lean from the tiers and benches,
> Cyclamen dripping and lilies.
> What fish-ways you have, littlest flowers,
> Swaying over the walks, in the watery air,
> Drowsing in soft light, petals pulsing.

With their "fish-ways" the flowers are infused with the progenitive
force of all life. The lost son's sexual beckoning ("Come," "Come
whispering," "Reach me," "Come, come," "Bend down") is full of
immense tension between psyche and nature, and the poet is strain-
ing for and desiring some overwhelming release. What results is an
ecstatic moment of visionary experience. The spirit struggling in
"the long alleys of string and stem" breaks into a moment of mys-
tical conjugation in which, as Hyatt Waggoner says, "the poet does
not so much 'ascend' as 'penetrate' by the power of his vision—
penetrate to the values inherent in experience."[13] In a rapturous
moment the lost son exclaims, "Light airs! Light airs! A pierce of
angels! / The leaves the leaves become me! / The tendrils have me!"
There is an ecstatic pain of penetration and an affirmation of the
immanence of the divine. This too, is a conjugal experience in which
the poet is enraptured by nature.

Similarly, in "A Field of Light" the lost son enters into dialogue
with nature's particulars. He moves from the deepest recesses of
submerged nature, "Under the blackened leaves" and "In the deep
grass," into a realm of polymorphously perverse delight: "Alone, I
kissed the skin of a stone; / Marrow-soft, danced in the sand." In
these moments of visionary experience which involve a *corre-
sponding activity* of self in nature and nature in self, Roethke's experi-
ence resembles Whitman's. Unlike Emerson, Waggoner maintains,

13. Hyatt H. Waggoner, *American Visionary Poetry* (Baton Rouge, 1982), 639.

Whitman does not tend to view nature as *maya;* rather, "his feeling for the individual, is tied to his stubborn, unrationalized sense that 'appearances' of experience must contain some kind of 'reality.' "[14]

In a way that recalls Whitman's breathless passion and pulsating sense of nature in section 2 of "Song of Myself," Roethke proclaims the inseparability of the cosmic and the minimal. As for Whitman, who knows "a leaf of grass is no less than the journey-work of the stars," there is for Roethke a similar democratic organicism in which the independent integrity of the minute particulars contains the meaning of the universe. With joyous understanding, the lost son exclaims:

> I could watch! I could watch!
> I saw the separateness of all things!
> My heart lifted up with the great grasses;
> The weeds believed me.

In Roethke's world of personification, "the weeds believe" because vision informs a faith that joins man in nature with nature in man. The movement from the illumined equality of particulars in nature into the expanse of the cosmos enables the lost son to affirm a confluence between self and the whole world: "I walked through the light air; / I moved with the morning."

Unlike the visionary excitation of "The Long Alley" and "A Field of Light," the culminating vision of "The Shape of the Fire" moves from a more childlike autoeroticism into a meditation. The lost son follows the light "further back / Into that minnowy world of weeds and ditches." Everything is turgid and expanding; the lines are long, sweeping, and cataloging, and the world is bathed by a growing light, "the full sun / Coming down on the flowerheads." The verbs are more passive and connote an intellectual process in which the poet comprehends and moves toward illumination by an intense observation of detail.

> To see cyclamen veins become clearer in early sunlight,
> And mist lifting out of the brown cat-tails;
> To stare into the after-light, the glitter left on the
>   lake's surface,

14. *Ibid.*, 644.

> When the sun had fallen behind a wooded island;
> To follow the drops sliding from a lifted oar,

The mind enters a Platonic realm and the metaphor moves from a cataloging openness into a more tightly controlled conceit. Light falling on nature is transformed into light falling into an opaque vase. The vase becomes the symbolic form and realm of mind where shape and form contain the world's motion. Then comes the moment of perfection in which the mind, the organic self, and nature are brought to an edge, and there motion and stasis meet. In this poised instant center and edge hold and three kinds of transparency—light (divine), water (nature), and opaque vase (mind) coincide, the self, "the contained flower," is held and fed, trembling in the unity of correspondence.

The final section of *Praise to the End!* continues Roethke's efforts to forge a way out of darkness, death, and stagnant waters. The poems affirm one of the major epistemological meanings of the entire sequence, that meaning and affirmation can exist only in the process, in the "going" which is endless. Every point of arrival is immediately undercut by the continual need to get lost again, a need for perpetual voyage.

The dramatic assertion of faith suggested by the title "Praise to the End!," which comes from "The Prelude," affirms the life journey and in an eschatological sense celebrates the end. Like "The Lost Son" and "Where Knock Is Open Wide," "Praise to the End!" is a poem of commencement. Beginning in that Dantean dark wood, Roethke's hero is once again lost and in despair. Here, the anguish is couched in predominantly sexual metaphors which distinguish this dark time from those of the two earlier poems as a more adult phase.

> It's dark in this wood, soft mocker.
> For whom have I swelled like a seed?
> What a bone-ache I have.
> Father of tensions, I'm down to my skin at last.

Whitman's gratifying autoeroticism is inverted. If, as Roethke has said, "onanism equals death" (PC, 40), then this masturbatory emptiness embodies an extreme condition of anguish and near mental breakdown ("swelled," "bone-ache," "tensions"). Mentally and phallically the lost son is at the end of his rope. This onanistic solipsism amplifies the need for sexual union and love: "Arch my back, pretty-bones, I'm dead at both ends." The emptiness after orgasm embodies the entirety of the protagonist's condition and his sense of the world; psychic, sexual, and natural rhythms are inseparable. Now, in darkness, "All risings / Fall."

Once more he recalls his innocence—"Once I fished from the banks, leaf-light and happy"—and then he reverts to a nursery chant that in its sexual playfulness is a release of frustration. All movement forward demands that he transcend masturbatory solipsism: "I'm undone by the flip-flap of odious pillows." Sexually spent, "An exact fall of waters has rendered me impotent," he awakes to his earthly sterility: "I've been asleep in a bower of dead skin."

In a familiar Roethkean way, the lost son must enact some form of phylogenetic evolution. Thus, before he can "feel more than a fish" and summon the spirit ("Ghost, come closer"), he exclaims: "Such owly pleasures! Fish come first, sweet bird." What follows is an ecstatic affirmation (always struggled for) similar to the joyous self of "O Lull Me, Lull Me" and "A Field of Light."

> I believe! I believe!—
> . . . .
> My ghosts are all gay.
> The light becomes me.

In the final three poems, the lost son is more conscious of the spirit's journey. The soul's unfolding requires an acceptance of the loss of prenatal innocence—"I can't crawl back through those veins"—and a recognition that "The field is no longer simple: / It's a soul's crossing time." The dialogue between the poet and the world intensifies. For the lost son, the world exists because of its own speech—a rhythm and a music that become one with the poet's process and the soul's journey. "Even thread had a speech," the lost son cries. Extending Whitman's belief in the holiness of animals and invoking the immanence of a consciousness and a poetic music in all things, the lost son beckons: "Sing, sing, you symbols! All simple creatures, / All small shapes, willow-shy, / In the obscure haze, sing!" In a way that is reminiscent of Whitman's belief that what society deems unclean is also holy, Roethke affirms that "All openings praise us, even oily holes."

Accepting the light within, "What grace I have is enough," the lost son moves to a quality of circularity in "I Cry, Love! Love!," which brings together an Emersonian Platonism with that twentieth-century "anguish of concreteness." Playing off of Emerson's "Circles," Roethke's persona asks, "Is circularity such a shame?" and completes the trope with a corresponding metaphor of concreteness. "A cat goes wider." Since he believes that spirit and matter are inseparable he can exclaim: "Hello, thingy spirit." As the poem opens up and anticipates the sweeping cataloging movements of "North American Sequence," everything moves in widening patterns and graceful flowing motions. "The bats weave in and out of the willows" and a "single wave starts lightly and easily shoreward." Out of a "gently rocking" sexual rhythm comes a coital joining in some prenatal past and, one might say, an affirmative answer to Hemingway's Nick Adams, who, knowing he must enter Big Two-Hearted River alone, chooses to turn back.

> We met in a nest. Before I lived.
> The dark hair sighed.
> We never enter
> Alone.

Metaphorically and euphonically the title of the last poem, "O, Thou Opening, O," suggests the importance of the circular shape. Like Emerson in "Uriel," who says, " 'Line in nature is not found;/ Unit and universe are round,' " the circle for Roethke embodies the eternal, the recurring shape of unity in the world, or to use Emerson's words, "the flying Perfect, around which the hands of man can never meet."[15] It is not only the eye, which for Emerson is the first circle, but the mouth—the orifice and organ of speech—which echoes the lost son's proclamation that "All openings praise us."

A sense of fragility and vulnerability underscores the ethereal nature of the poem. The suggestion of the Crucifixion in the opening inaugurates the dematerializing nature of the self: "I'll make it; but it may take me. /. . . My left side's tender. / Read me the stream." For the first time there is a conspicuous absence of sense, vegetal life, and marshlike landscape. Rather, a quality of elevated

15. Emerson, *Selected Writings*, 280.

lightness characterizes the lost son's mind: "I'm a draft sleeping by a stick; / I'm lost in what I have." The world is resplendent with those aspects of nature that embody the spirit: wind, sky, light. In the prose poem opening of section 2, everything in the natural world is covered with a haze of holy spirit, a glimmering etherealness.

And now are we to have that pelludious Jesus-shimmer over all things, the animal's candid gaze, a shade less than feathers, light's broken speech revived, a ghostly going of tame bears, a bright moon on gleaming skin, a thing you cannot say to whisper and equal a Wound?

A presence of spirit transforms the lost son, and he reminds himself, "A leaf could drag you," before he goes the way of air's essence.

Oh, what a webby wonder I am!
Swaying, would you believe,
Like a sapling tree,
Enough to please a cloud!

Here Roethke follows the Transcendentalist tradition of Emerson, Whitman, and Dickinson, who in order to transcend the self must distill the purest elements of the atmosphere and intoxicate the soul. One recalls Whitman drunk on the "odorless atmosphere" in "Song of Myself," or Dickinson, that "inebriate of air" or "debauchee of dew," in "I taste a liquor never brewed," or even Emerson in "Bacchus," asking for "wine which never grew / In the belly of the grape." So, too, Roethke in his postmodern way concocts a version of that radical American impulse which demands self-transcendence through a distillation of the invisible.

Emerson's first opening, the eye, which for Roethke brings together the seer and the seen—God and man—calls the lost son forth: "An Eye says, / Come." The self continues to dematerialize, to grow lighter, more delicate, intoxicated by atmosphere and light ("I'm twinkling like a twig!"). Body and spirit are united in the lost son's world, and transcendence is not a denial of self: "This flesh has airy bones." The sequence closes in an open-ended way, affirming the meaning of the entire journey.

Going is knowing.
I see; I seek;

I'm near.
Be true,
Skin.

As he would later say in "The Waking," "What falls away is always. And is near." Here what is "near" joins seeing and seeking—the poet is always moving toward some form of knowing which is close but still far because the tension must remain perpetual.

FIVE

The Love Poems

The evolution of the poems and the growth of the man were always intertwined. Significant personal events provided Roethke with a dramatic center that would become a chrysalis for his metaphor. Whereas a childhood spent in his father's greenhouse, his father's death, and his mental breakdowns were the chief personal events standing behind *The Lost Son* and *Praise to the End!*, his marriage to Beatrice O'Connell on January 3, 1953, was the major event of the next phase of his poetry.

At the center of the new poems Roethke included in *Words for the Wind* (1958) are the "Love Poems." The theme of love and self-transcendence through love dominates the new developments in his poetry of the fifties. Although there are fewer of them, the "Love Poems," like the poems of *Praise to the End!*, are written compulsively and obsessively. Here, too, rhythm, metaphor, and trope overlap and grow out of one another.

Like Petrarch, Spenser, Shakespeare, and Donne, who record love's progress in an unfolding group or series of poems, Roethke charts a journey into love. But unlike Petrarch, for example, who conceives of love as an idealizing passion, Roethke sees it as a natural passion of body, mind, and soul. He would agree with Lucretius that love is "a primary function of the animate universe and essential to its continuance"[1] and with Whitman that love is the power which unites the universe. Roethke believes in love as an active, driving force, the passion of human life that joins not only man and woman but man and nature, body and soul, human self with deity.

1. Lu Emily Pearson, *Elizabethan Love Conventions* (New York, 1966), 6.

In these poems of the mid-fifties, Roethke joins the great love poets for whom "love opens for the soul new gates to new worlds."[2] And in this new world of love, the mind feels, the soul thinks, and the body knows. Written in the aftermath of Roethke's marriage, the poems are certainly a kind of epithalamium. Yet they are more than a celebration of marriage, for they probe the very life-driving nature of love—sexually, psychologically, and spiritually. The "Love Poems" mark another stage of growth in the lost son's journey out of the self. The old adage that one cannot love another until one loves oneself applies well to the lost son. Only after the struggle to achieve some human identity in *The Lost Son* and *Praise to the End!* can the lost son face the joys, problems, and complexities of human love in *Words for the Wind.*

The "Love Poems" are characterized by a point of transformation where human passion becomes spiritual passion, and erotic play and sexual joining merge with the soul's drama. Love for Roethke, who once said, "I'm sick of women. I want God" (SF, 112), seems always infused with spiritual drive. Louis Martz's remark that for Donne "the lover of women and the lover of God are not separable"[3] applies to Roethke as well. And given Roethke's spiritual proclivity it is helpful at times to view the love poems within a mystical context. I do not mean to suggest that Roethke is a Christian or a mystic, but rather that he is a poet for whom the dynamics of Christian mysticism have poetic value.

The act of love, Underhill claims, lies at the heart of mysticism, and the fundamental difference between magic and mysticism is that "magic wants to get, mysticism wants to give." The mystical experience, she continues, is

> essentially a movement of the heart, seeking to transcend the limitations of the individual standpoint and to surrender itself to ultimate reality; for no personal gain . . . but purely for an instinct of love. By the word heart, of course we mean here not merely "the seat of the affections," "the organ of tender emotion," and the life: but rather the inmost sanctuary of personal being, the deep root of its love and will, the very source of its energy and life. The mystic is "in love with the Absolute" not in any

2. *Ibid.*, 11.
3. Louis Martz, *The Wit of Love* (South Bend, Ind., 1969), 31.

idle or sentimental manner, but in that vital sense which presses at all costs and through all dangers toward union with the object beloved.[4]

The writings of the mystics reveal the inseparable relationship between literary expression and religious experience. In their search to find some means of human expression to communicate what is ultimately ineffable, the mystics have found that metaphoric language, especially paradox and oxymoron, is often the only kind of language they can use. More than several Christian mystics, among them St. Augustine, St. John of the Cross, St. Theresa, and St. Catherine of Siena, have written fine poetry and moving poetical prose. Underhill's observation of the relationship between mysticism, love, and the music of song applies as well to poetic experience: "The condition of joyous and awakened love to which the mystic passes when his purification is at an end is to him, above all else, the state of Song. He does not 'see' the spiritual world: he 'hears' it. For him, as for St. Francis of Assisi, it is a 'heavenly melody, intolerably sweet.' "[5]

This heavenly melody is fundamental to that rhythmic element of poetry which transforms the poem, at its highest level, to pure song. Hence, Roethke's discovery of love enables him to hear the meaning of love in his lover's voice and in the music of poetry. In "The Voice," he hears in his lover's "low voice . . . / More than a mortal should."

Both in subject matter and in their more formal structure, the new poems of *The Waking* (1953) and *Words for the Wind* (1958) mark a break with the poems of the previous two volumes. In various notebook entries from the fifties, Roethke reveals a sense of having exhausted something with the completion of *Praise to the End!* and a need to move in a new direction. It is "the mark of the true poet," he notes, "that he perpetually renews himself" (SF, 261). No doubt referring to the psychic shape of the long poems, he says "a writer can get trapped in a form, in a psychological stance, an attitude, and he must struggle, often, to extricate himself or he may die" (SF, 255).

The problem of where to go after the achievement of *The Lost Son* and *Praise to the End!* is, as much as anything, a technical problem. Roethke's new concern with love and self-transcendence and with a

4. Evelyn Underhill, *Mysticism* (New York, 1955), 70, 71–72.
5. *Ibid.*, 77.

somewhat more metaphysical notion of reality leads him to a more formal poetic structure: "Form acts the father: tells you what you may and may not do" (SF, 255). He becomes more interested in the line as a poetic unit than he had been in the past: "To make the line in itself interesting, syntactically, that is the problem" (SF, 260). In these new poems, the line assumes much of the poetic responsibility that the naive language, intuitive syntax, and "telescopic" metaphor previously carried. Against the more formal restrictions of the line, Roethke sets his lyricism and generates a verbal intensity through which love's transformations are dramatized. Although this lyrically intensified line is reminiscent of Yeats—critics have called this period of Roethke's work his Yeatsian phase—these poems are not imitative. On the contrary, the poet here is working at the height of his powers, absorbing elements of the tradition into his own sensibility. When Roethke takes his "cadence from a man named Yeats" and gives "it back again," he gives it back with the cadence transformed.

"Four for Sir John Davies" is a major poem of departure. If the poems of The Lost Son and Praise to the End! are about a ceaseless struggle to be born, "Four for Sir John Davies" is then a kind of overture to the lost son's waking to a world in which the possibility of human love exists. Having attained some kind of human identity, he is capable of facing the human and divine meaning of love. The four sections of the poem are, in a musical sense, four movements that open into each other and comprise a process by which the poet is able to begin to fathom the dimensions of love. The mind's movement, the cadence of poetry, the rhythm of the body in erotic play and sexual love, and the motion of the seeking spirit are all part of Roethke's expansive notion of love.

In the first section, "The Dance," Roethke finds a common metaphor which joins the mind, emotion, and poetic imagination with the body and the soul. The dance is rhythm—or, literally translated from the Greek, measured movement—and for the poet perhaps there is nothing more universal and essentially unitive than the measured movement of (all things in) process. Rhythm is for a poet like Roethke a common poetic experience of life. It is this dance "slowing in the mind of man" which enables the poet to find some "still turning point," to use Eliot's phrase, where temporal and eternal experience are brought to a point of conjunction. Implicit in such a rhythmic notion of reality is a simultaneous quest for order and a creative need for chaos. Poetically, the very formal harnessing of the rhythms of this primal dance embodies the struggle between order and chaos that lies at the heart of Roethke's experiences of love.

In "The Dance," the mind's ordering movement slows reality so the poet can apprehend some universal cadence.

> Is that dance slowing in the mind of man
> That made him think the universe could hum?
> The great wheel turns its axle when it can;

For Roethke, the imaginative mind's movement and the rhythm of the whole universe cannot be separated; the same "slow / Wheel of the stars," which the young boy saw in the night sky in "Double Feature," he now imagines as being one with the mind. In identifying with the "romping" bears, Roethke sees his large and clumsy self set free. He seeks some harmonious way to be in the world—an "animal remembering to be gay."

Such animal movement unites the imagination with the world outside. The "caged bear rarely does the same thing twice" because the animal movement in the mind and the dancing animal in the world are joined, and in the imagination they create the world anew each time. Roethke's comic assertion, "O watch his body sway!" foreshadows the lover who will later learn to "measure time by how a body sways." This dance which begins in solitude, "all alone," involves a human speech, a poetry that must teach the "toes to listen to my tongue." Whereas in *Praise to the End!* the "motion of a stone" would have consummated a momentary marriage between the poet and the world, here it is only "joyless" and is not enough. To be "dancing-mad" as only the poet would know—as Yeats, the master of this cadence, would know—has to do with what exists between imagination, the human heart, and the desire for another.

In the next section, "The Partner," the poet ventures forth from his solitary dancing. His desire involves both sexual need and the human responsibility "to make someone else complete." Dazzled by his lover, whose passion "would set sodden straw on fire," he wonders if he was "the servant of a sovereign wish." Since the rhythm of the two lovers in sexual play and the cadence of poetry are inseparable, to play "a measure with commingled feet" is, for the punning poet-lover, the making of metrical feet as well as the touching of toes. In this wild excitement of bodily love, there is a miraculous awakening to the power of passion and a fusion of flesh and blood: "She kissed me close, and then did something else. / My marrow beat as wildly as my pulse."

For this bearish lover, the passion of physical love leads beyond the flesh. Like Whitman, who claims a parity for body and soul and brings together transcendent experience with sexual union so that spirit and flesh are part and parcel of each other, Roethke proclaims that "the spirit knows the body head to toe." "The body is the soul," as he once said in a notebook entry. In "The Partner," the ravished lover swears this fact of life: "I'd say it to my horse: we live beyond / Our outer skin." Roethke, with Donne and Whitman, believes that when the spirit's motion and the body's rhythm join, love can arrest the temporal measure by which we live. Returning such love brings the lover closer to the immaterial and wakes the spirit: "I gave her kisses back, and woke a ghost."

Because to wake the ghost is to arouse the spirit, the lovers' sexual joining becomes a drive toward the divine. In this pure and innocent realm where "body and the soul know how to play," the lovers enter a "dark world where gods have lost their way." Like Dante's Beatrice, Roethke's partner leads him toward salvation. In accord with the mystic, the poet must lose himself if he is to find his true self and knowledge of the Absolute.

In the section "The Wraith" the transformation of sexual love into spiritual love becomes an urge toward transcendence and union with the Absolute. R. C. Zaehner's relation of sex to the sacred applies to Roethke, for the sexual act, Zaehner asserts, is "the one act of which man is capable that makes him like God both in the intensity of his union with his partner and in the fact that by this union he is a co-creator with god."[6] The dancing lovers enter a world of "Incomprehensible gaiety and dread" where "the two eternal

6. Geoffrey Parrinder, *Mysticism in the World's Religions* (New York, 1976), 171.

passions of the self, the desire of love and the desire of knowledge," co-exist.[7] For Roethke, as for those metaphysical lovers Shakespeare and Donne, love is that singular experience in which body and soul are joined in human communion and wordly time is transcended.

In this world of change and death, Roethke's proclamation seems an affirmative reply to Hamlet's difficulty in "taking arms against a sea of troubles." The poet and his lover pit themselves against mortality and the flux of time: "We two, together, on a darkening day / Took arms against our own obscurity." With a metaphysical wit, he unveils his idea of love's knowledge. "Behind" and "before" refer not only to the time before and after orgasm, but to a corresponding metaphysical notion of time. It is only in the act of union that "the lonely pastures of the dead" are obliterated.

The surrendering of one self to another is sexual, spiritual, and metaphysical; such union generates a purity and innocence necessary if the transcendent world of love is to be realized. Hence, Roethke's notion of sexual "play" involves the kind of liberating innocence which returns the lovers to a primal state of innocence and harmony—the childlike condition essential to the transcendent experience.

> Did each become the other in that play?
> She laughed me out, and then she laughed me in;
> In the deep middle of ourselves we lay;
> When glory failed, we danced upon a pin.
> The valley rocked beneath the granite hill;
> Our souls looked forth, and the great day stood still.

The pure play of coital rhythm is the merging and exchange of being—a momentary dissolution of selfhood that involves a faith in the other. Such interpenetration opens the lovers to a rhythm of the world; like angels, they "danced upon a pin," and "The valley rocked beneath the granite hill." They recover a prelapsarian state, an Eden where, in "the rich weather of a dappled wood / We played with dark and light as children should."

With the recovery of this original world of "dark and light," the lovers move toward a state of mystical intensity where everything is elemental and original—"Sea-beast or bird flung toward the rav-

7. Martz, *The Wit of Love*, 72.

aged shore." In love's ascent ("We rose to meet the moon, and saw no more"), reality is transformed and the poet's love appears as a vision, a wraith of light. Since for Roethke divine "knowledge lives in paradox" (SF, 225), he says here "It was and was not she, a shape alone, / Impaled on light, and whirling slowly down." Not only is she being and nothingness but, in a mystical sense, both lovers are "Impaled"; she is transfixed by light and he is momentarily transfixed, stunned and overcome by her radiance and omnipotence as she comes "whirling" down.

"The Vigil," the last section, is a night watch in the mind—a meditation on this mystery of love. Once again Roethke brings together the poet's solitary dance of section 1 (the sexual union of "The Partner") and the visionary experience of "The Wraith." Like Dante's Beatrice, Roethke's Beatrice shows him "hidden virtue without flaw," and now in this aftermath the poet must confirm its meaning. Thus, "The Vigil" in its confirmation of love brings the journey of love's dance to a new level of meaning.

Since Roethke often had Eliot on his mind, his affirmative cry can be seen as an answer to the sterility and resignation that leave Prufrock unable to summon the mermaids "riding seaward on the waves / Combing the white hair" of the water. Roethke's man of love asserts: "The waves broke easy, cried to me in white; / Her look was morning in the dying light." The dance, the universal rhythm of love, brings Roethke to the *via affirmativa*.[8] The dance in the mind and the universe on its axle continue to hum and turn in a rhythm that also embodies the "Rapt" lovers whose dancing "mocked before the black / And shapeless night that made no answer back." In mocking this shapeless night, Roethke also says no, it seems to me, to those "meaningless plungings of water and the wind" which define Stevens' world in "The Idea of Order at Key West."

In the sense that mysticism is pure love and wants to give and, finally, give up the self to the "other," Roethke can only die to his lover in the fullest way: "Alive at noon, I perished in her form." This ultimately unitive experience involves a most complex intertwining

8. See Hyatt H. Waggoner, *American Poets: From Puritanism to the Present* (Baton Rouge, 1984), 637–56, for a definition of the *via affirmativa* as a strain in western mysticism that emphasizes the individual's ability to retain the world during mystical experience rather than negate it as, say, St. John of the Cross does.

of rhythms; poetry, mind, body, and spirit all merge and allow the lovers to transcend the flesh: "Who rise from flesh to spirit know the fall: / The word outleaps the world, and light is all." For Roethke, "word" and "light" are religious and aesthetic. The "Word," as St. John tells us (1:14–18), is the truth made flesh in Jesus and "true light" is the fact of his dwelling among us. Although Roethke is not being doctrinally Christian here, his metaphor resonates with spiritual meaning for "word" and "light" affirm ultimate truth and the transcendence of worldly time love can bring us. Yet "word" and "light" signify, as well, the light of the imagination and the immutability of poetry itself. The poet embraces the eternity that language gives to timeless human emotion in its struggle to overcome change and flux.

"The Dream," which inaugurates the sequence of "Love Poems" in *Words for the Wind*, reveals the lost son's unconscious mind in a more humanized light than in "Give Way, Ye Gates," where the mind's deep stream remembers that "Once I was a pond." Here, Roethke's "deeper sleep" recalls his lover's sensual form which wakes him to the world: "Eye learned from eye, cold lip from sensual lip." Love, for Roethke, always moves outward, confirming some relationship between the self, the lover, nature, and finally the divine.

In "The Dream," love creates the very elements of the world; earth, air, fire, and water become the embodiment of love's passion. The poet's vision of his lover activates the elements so that nature and supernature are in constant interchange and oscillation: "My dream divided on a point of fire; / . . . The water rippled, and she rippled on." He moves with creation because the world moves in and out of his lover. She transforms the world and is in turn transformed. As the moon illuminates her in the dark, earth and air are charged with an awesome force. Everything is electric, the air undulates with his lover's movement, the night is on fire with unnatural light. Dynamic form in perfection, she sets the earth in motion: "The bushes and the stones danced on and on." Like the air, she is moving and is everywhere.

The lost son's growth into love involves the ability to give one's self to another and accept the responsibility of being loved. There is thus something human as well as transcendent in this poem. Coburn Freer likens Roethke to the prodigal son who died when he left his loved ones and to be reborn had to return to accept the responsibility of being loved.[9] To a certain degree this lies at the heart of the humanizing experience that love's journey must be. The poet, knowing that "Love is not love until love's vulnerable," can find in love the world's motion, a way to rejoin humanity and nature: "She knew the grammar of least motion, she / Lent me one virtue, and I live thereby."

In this dream, his lover assumes what Roethke would later call "the pure poise of the spirit." Love's unitive force is transformed into the immaterial; she is love, she is the *spiritus mundi* holding "her body steady in the wind," joining and forming the world—air, earth, fire, and water. Roethke's use of oxymoron brings the power of love into the realm of the natural and supernatural at once: the lovers "slowly swung around," and, fusing the cosmic with the sexual, the poet plays "in flame and water like a boy" and "like a wet log . . . sang within a flame." At the most incomprehensible limits of love, order and form coexist with the illimitable so that in apprehending "eternity's confine" the vulnerable lover can say, "I came to love, I came into my own."

To "come into" love is to rejoin the world with a new heart and rejoice with creation. The title of "All the Earth, All the Air" may very well have been inspired by the same stanza of Christopher Smart's "Song to David" from which Roethke took "where knock is open wide." As the poet journeys into love, he finds that love involves not only the struggle with one's identity but also a surrendering of part of the self and an acceptance of the other. Thus, faith and love are inseparable, for the heart's knowledge involves both passions. What for Smart pertains to the man of prayer, pertains with equal intensity to Roethke's man of love.

> But stronger still, in earth and air,
> And in the sea, the man of prayer,
> And far beneath the Tide.
> In the seat of faith assign'd,

9. Coburn Freer, "Theodore Roethke's Love Poetry," *Northwest Review*, XI (Summer, 1971), 67–69.

Where ask is have, where seek is find,
Where knock is open wide.
(Christopher Smart, "Song of David")

When Roethke proclaims in stanza 2 "This joy's my fall. I am!," he knows that love affirms a kind of ultimate life but involves a fall from solipsistic innocence into a world where the painful struggles between lovers comprise one part of love's fullness. Sexually and humanly, the lost son now can "stand with standing stones." He finds the world overcome with the fullness of his love, which paradoxically reverses nature: "The blossom stings the bee." To come to love is to come into one's own only by recognizing the meaning of the fall and the damnation of a world without love—a world without the complex responsibilities of giving oneself and denying selfhood. Roethke's closing recognition, "What's hell but a cold heart? / But who, faced with her face, / Would not rejoice?," recalls St. Paul's famous passage on love (1 Cor. 13): "For now we see in a mirror dimly, but then face to face. . . . So faith, hope, love abide, these three; but the greatest of these is love." Roethke's allusion to the Pauline trope of seeing "face to face" is not, of course, Christian in meaning. Rather, it conveys the poet's feeling that human love is also an ultimate confrontation. Faced with his love's face he no longer sees "in a mirror dimly."

"Words for the Wind" confirms this growth. The world is charged with the presence of love. What was metaphysical in "Four for Sir John Davies" is now rooted in nature, and the poet begins to comprehend the vastness of love in terms of beauty and form in motion. Love is active and, as Roethke says, "has a thing to do." No longer a child of the primal world of water and rock as in *Praise to the End!*, he exclaims: "I smile, no mineral man; / I bear, but not alone, / The burden of this joy."

This fall into love where burden and joy are inseparable is less mythical than the fall in "The Vigil." Such love brings body and spirit together and involves the human, natural, and metaphysical worlds. Echoing his notebook assertion that "only the mad know the extravagances of love" (SF, 215), he says, "I'm odd and full of love." And because love and faith are inseparable, "Those who embrace, believe." For St. Paul "love bears all things," and for

Roethke "All things bring me to love." Accepting the burden of love's joy, he can bare himself to another and say:

> And I dance round and round,
> A fond and foolish man,
> And see and suffer myself
> In another being, at last.

In one sense, the sequence builds to "I Knew a Woman," which is not only a pivotal poem but also one of Roethke's finest achievements. His journey toward "another being, at last" has almost obsessively involved nature, supernature, and dream. Physically and spiritually, "knowing" and "woman" are brought together, and the meaning of love unfolds for the poet in a new way. For Roethke, sexual union and mystical illumination are inseparable ways of knowing. His lover is more than a dazzling lover, she is a lover in the flesh and in the spirit—a kind of houri who embodies nature and supernature; she creates a world in which body and soul rise into each other, affirming a greater unitive act which brings man beyond self and time into the eternal.

Here, more than ever, the multiple facets of love are contained in his lover's terrific energy and motion, in her transformative ways. The primal force and the transcendent movement of the poem are held in tension by a formal structure; the four rhyming stanzas, $a\ b\ a\ b\ c\ c\ c$, embody the poet's creative struggle to harness the illimitable and to give passion the lyrical intensity it demands. The genius of conceit and the spiraling repetition of imagery and metaphor enable the lovers and the poem to move, as he says in the poem, "more ways than one."

> I knew a woman, lovely in her bones,
> When small birds sighed, she would sigh back at them;
> Ah, when she moved, she moved more ways than one:
> The shapes a bright container can contain!
> Of her choice virtues only gods should speak,
> Or English poets who grew up on Greek
> (I'd have them sing in chorus, cheek to cheek).

A creator of a dance that is in "the mind of man" and in the body of the world, this woman sighing back at small birds knows the innocence of nature, and here the poet takes his cadence from her.

She returns us to the purity of Greek tragedy—to a time when poetry and dance were a fertility rite deemed essential for procreation and survival. She is Nietzsche's dythrambic dancer worshiped by those "English poets who grew up on Greek." Playing more than a "measure with commingled feet," she is dancer, teacher, muse. In an Elizabethan way, Roethke's punning is humorous, witty, and bawdy. The suggestion of formal turns of the Greek chorus on stage (strophe, antistrophe, and epode) is also the titillation of sexual foreplay and the lovers' positioning in bed.

> How well her wishes went! She stroked my chin,
> She taught me Turn, and Counter-turn, and Stand;
> She taught me Touch, that undulant white skin;
> I nibbled meekly from her proffered hand;
> She was the sickle; I, poor I, the rake,
> Coming behind her for her pretty sake
> (But what prodigious mowing we did make).

In a motion that reaches beyond itself, she becomes "undulant white skin" and the poet a humble knight in a courtly romance, following the leads of his love and obediently serving her wishes. This fertility dance becomes a "prodigious mowing." The conceit is many faceted. She is shape and motion; she is the sickle, the gracefully curved, half-moon-shaped scythe (a shape symbolic of fertility) which cuts the crop at seed. The poet is the rake (Roethke plays on both meanings), the dandyish Don Juan humbled and overwhelmed by this beauty and the phallic-shaped, harvesting rake. In "Coming behind her for her pretty sake," Roethke puns on the sexual positioning of their dance in bed and on his chivalrous love. This reformed profligate must come "behind," or after her, so that she may reach climax first.

Notwithstanding Roethke's continual punning—"gander" and "goose" referring to male and female, look and touch—love continues to move toward the realm of the spirit. Although "her full lips pursed, the errant note to seize" playfully suggests oral sex, the chivalrous sense of "errant" continues the poet's transformation from a dandy to a knight on a spiritual quest. The poem moves into a paradox where extreme motion and stillness coexist, and we move, appropriately, into a transcendent reality. Thus, while her "knees" are "flowing," her "several parts could keep a pure repose." She moves and the poet moves beyond the Platonic world of Emerson's circles into a world where pure form is itself energized: "(She moved in circles, and those circles moved)."

The circular movement continues, and the cyclical time of the seasons, the phases of nature's growth, bring Roethke and his lover, as sickle and rake, into a world where knowing love involves a liberation of the self from desire and worldly time. Courtly love becomes the saint's humility and resignation to the other.

> Let seed be grass, and grass turn into hay:
> I'm martyr to a motion not my own;
> What's freedom for? To know eternity.
> I swear she cast a shadow white as stone.
> But who would count eternity in days?
> These old bones live to learn her wanton ways:
> (I measure time by how a body sways).

The paradox intensifies in a mystical way, so that what Roethke meant when he said "he that lives by the skin will die in it" (SF, 191) becomes clear. Dark and light combine as her shadow transfixes him. The conjunction of body and spirit brings Roethke to a kind of self-effacement which enables him to move beyond the time of days. In this realm, time becomes motion, the transcendent power of love's rhythm, swaying with body and soul.

In the next three poems, "The Voice," "She," and "The Other," the force of love becomes the source of poetry. Roethke uses the familiar Romantic metaphor of the bird as nature's purest singer of poetry. In Roethke's world, "knowing" a woman involves the mystery of poetic utterance itself; the bird's song and his lover's voice are irrevocably joined. His lover becomes a muse, a singer of music in the world who defines his life and makes possible his craft. Like Whitman and Keats, Roethke defines the poet as a "solitary singer" who, when he enters the deep regions of nature, can hear those Emersonian "primal warblings." To be a solitary singer, the poet must himself find the silence and solitude in which he can hear the bird alone; he must return to an original condition where the imagination and nature are one, and where, to recall Emerson, "the air is music and the poet . . . is caught up into the life of the Universe. . . . and his words are universally intelligible as the plants and animals."[10]

Whitman says of the bird who returns him to his true self, "O wondrous singer! / You only I hear," and Keats's nightingale who was heard only in "ancient days by emperor and clown" tolls him "back" to his "sole self." In a post-Romantic sense, the bird song of Roethke's muse-lover is less melodious and full than that of Keats and Whitman. Roethke hears a "thin song," "Diminished, yet still heard." Like Whitman's hermit thrush, this "shy cerulean bird" beckons the poet at once out of himself and into a deep recess of himself. Thus, he can affirm poetry's unifying "open sound, / Aloft, and on the ground."

Also, evoking Whitman's trinity of "lilac, star, and bird" "twined to the chant" of his soul, Roethke's trinity of "Bird, girl, and ghostly tree" join love, poetry, and the soul and unite "earth" and "solid air." Poetry transforms life into a fecund season. Like Keats's nightingale singing of "summer in full-throated ease," Roethke becomes a singer of life's ripe season: "Their slow song sang in me; / The long noon pulsed away, / Like any summer day."

In "She," his lady laughs, "delighting in what is." As her voice incorporates the meaning of poetry's song: "She lilts a low soft language, and I hear / Down long sea-chambers of the inner ear." Her voice is not only a primal warbling but is also a part of the pulse of the daily world, and he feels "her presence in the common day." Because "She knows the speech of light, and makes it plain," she is able to transform the divine into the universally intelligible and into the pure natural diction of poetry.

Finally, in "The Other," his lover becomes something numinous. Her poetic truth is more than the body's motion transcending time; it is the timeless music of poetry of which she is, in part, the source. To be a sinner is to be a lover: "Is she what I become? / Is this my final Face? / I find her every place." Like the loafing Whitman, he declares himself "A Lazy natural man, / I loll, I loll, all Tongue." Because she is eros, spirit, and singer, and he can love her, he affirms something like what Whitman called in "Lilacs" "death's outlet song of life."

10. Ralph Waldo Emerson, *The Selected Writings*, ed. Brooks Atkinson (New York, 1950), 84.

Roethke sobs at the end of the poem, "Aging, I sometimes weep, / Yet still laugh in my sleep."

"The Pure Fury" and "The Renewal" mark the poet's culminating surge toward love's purity and ultimately toward salvation. Here, the meaning of love is best understood in terms of mystical experience. What Underhill says of mysticism pertains to the struggle in these poems: "True mystical achievement is the most complete and difficult of life. . . . it is at once an act of love, an act of surrender, and an act of supreme perception; a trinity of experience which meets and satisfies the three activities of the self."[11] Here the love of a woman and the love of the Absolute become inseparable, and Roethke's struggle, like that of the saint, is to face the necessity of surrendering the self: "Parmenides put Nothingness in place; / She tries to think, and it flies loose again." This mystical love which brings Roethke face to face with nothingness leads him to the Creator by way of the paradoxes of creation. Creation is a pure fury in which chaos has a kind of order. The plurality and change of Parmenides' phenomenal world and the immutability of Plato's forms, in a sense, harness each other. Only Roethke's Beatrice can bring him to this creation and its purgative power.

For the lover as mystic, the "terrible . . . need for solitude" brings the poet to the brink of nonbeing where love and death are forms of the same Absolute. The need for solitude is a need to purify the will's misguided desire.

> How terrible the need for solitude:
> That appetite for life so ravenous
> A man's a beast prowling in his own house,
> A beast with fangs, and out for his own blood
> Until he finds the thing he almost was
> When the pure fury first raged in his head
> And trees came closer with a denser shade.

Like the double self of Delmore Schwartz's "heavy bear," Roethke struggles with that libidinal appetite that keeps him from the pure. This anguished need for purification is an act of self-effacement which becomes a rite of self-devouring. He must be "out for his own

11. Underhill, *Mysticism*, 84.

blood" before he can find that cleansing source of fury, that primordial imagination—the dense shade of the Garden.

This Roethkean world of love, sex, and death holds two means of losing the self in an act of transcendence which leads to nothingness, or God, who is no-thing-ness.

> Dream of a woman, and dream of death:
> The light air takes my being's breath away;
> I look on white, and it turns into gray—
> When will that creature give me back my breath?

In a notebook entry Roethke echoes the mystic's feeling that "despair and the most transcendental love of God are inseparable" (SF, 190). Having experienced something transcendent and having been brought to love's divine power, he plunges into the terror of his own finitude. The poem opens in a state of negation and misery not unlike what St. John of the Cross describes as the dark night of the soul.

> The Dark Night, then, is really a deeply human process, in which the self which thought itself so spiritual, so firmly established upon the supersensual plane, is forced to turn back, to leave the Light, and pick up those qualities which it had let behind. Only thus, by the transmutation of the whole man, not by a careful and departmental cultivation of that which we like to call his "spiritual" side, can Divine Humanity be formed. . . . A new and more drastic purgation is needed—not of the organs of perception, but of the very shrine of the self: that "heart" which is the seat of personality, the source of its love and will. In the stress and anguish of the Night, when it turns back from the vision of the Infinite to feel again the limitations of the finite, the self loses the power to Do.[12]

In "The Pure Fury," Roethke faces this part of the self and the need for drastic purgation.

> Stupor of knowledge lacking inwardness—
> What book, O learned man, will set me right?
> Once I read nothing through a fearful night,
> For every meaning had grown meaningless.

The self not only needs solitude for this kind of purification, but it must face the terror of nothingness which is both the emptiness of

12. *Ibid.*, 388–89.

self and the possibility of apprehending the divine. As Underhill
says, "When St. Paul saw nothing, he saw God."[13] For Roethke, to
"love a woman with an empty face" is to reckon with the love of the
Absolute and, in a sense, to love God as the saint does.

> The pure admire the pure, and live alone;
> I love a woman with an empty face.
>
> . . . .
>
> I live near the abyss. I hope to stay
> Until my eyes look at a brighter sun
> As the thick shade of the long night comes on.

His lover becomes that substance, that which overwhelms him,
renders him a stunned, surrendering man who risks himself to live
near "the abyss" where being and nothingness merge and the pure
fury of creation is pitted against the soul's moral dereliction, "As the
thick shade of the long night comes on."

The movement is similar in "The Renewal." From the "Motions of
the soul" which affirm the "perpetual" and enable Roethke's love
sighs "to lengthen into songs," he falls into a dark night. Once more
he is a lost son: "The night wind rises. Does my father live?" In a
world of genesis where "Dark hangs upon the waters of the soul,"
the poet whose "flesh is breathing slower than a wall" confronts
that anguish of annihilation necessary for love's will to turn toward
the spirit. "Love alters all," he cries, "Unblood my instinct, love."
Out of these drowsy Keatsian waters of the psyche, Roethke moves
toward the spirit of the wind.

Paradoxically, Roethke's "Sudden renewal of the self" occurs in
the darkest hour. Sapped of everything, "A raw ghost drinks the
fluid in my spine," he enters that depth of the dark night which St.
John says is characterized by fatigue and lassitude—"a dreadful
ennui, a dull helplessness."[14] A lost man who cries, "I know I love,
yet know not where I am," endures by faith alone.

In an affirmation of resignation and self-acceptance, he says in
the last section:

> Dry bones! Dry bones! I find my loving heart,
> Illumination brought to such a pitch

13. *Ibid.*, 400.
14. *Ibid.*, 400–401.

> I see the rubblestones begin to stretch
> As if reality had split apart
> And the whole motion of the soul lay bare:
> I find that love, and I am everywhere.

After the dark night, the truth of the loving heart is illumination. The poet is cleansed by a vision of creation—the elemental world beginning to move. Rendering the naked soul to the whole is a supreme love, "that *fiat voluntas tua* which marks the death of self-hood in the interests of a new and deeper life." Having found a way from "multiplicity to Unity," the lost soul rejoins the world to proclaim: "I find that love, and I am everywhere." In the final poems of the sequence, the lost son affirms his return. Capable of accepting the burden of loving and being loved, in "The Swan" he playfully rejoices: "I am my father's son, I am John Donne / Whenever I see her with nothing on." And in the final poem, "Memory," he sings this knowledge to the world: "The wind dies on the hill. / Love's all. Love's all I know."

SIX

The Mask and Its Cracks: The Old Woman's Meditations

Before he had completed *Words for the Wind* in 1957, Roethke was becoming fixated on death. It is clear that his ailing body had something to do with this. As early as 1953, when he and Beatrice were living in Rome, where he was teaching on a Ford Foundation Fellowship, he was suffering from severe hypertension. In a letter to Kenneth Burke shortly after his return from Europe he writes: "I went steadily through the restaurants and country houses (one) only to arrive home with a blood-pressure of 205–210 and landsickness. The latter has disappeared. But I still feel woozy from these wonder-drugs used to bring down the blood pressure. And for the first time a wee bit concerned at the collapsing physical mechanism" (SL, 194). And he mentions the same condition to William Werner early in 1953: "When I got off the boat, I had a blood-pressure of 205, but now it's way down to 130–140. And my liver, kidneys, and heart are all undamaged, I learn after a lot of fancy testing" (SL, 198). This new awareness of his declining physical condition had something to do with his move away from the ecstatic lyrics of the "Love Poems" that had defined much of *Words for the Wind.*

Furthermore, having written himself out of the kind of metaphysical lyric that characterized the "Love Poems" he felt the need to move, technically, in a new direction. In a letter to Ralph J. Mills, he explains his desire to bring together a meditative style with a new dramatic impulse in the sequence he would call "Meditations of An Old Woman": "As for the old lady poems, I wanted (1) to create a character for whom such rhythms are indigenous; that she be a dramatic character, not just me. Christ, Eliot in the Quartets is tired, spiritually tired, old-man. Rhythm, Tiresome Tom. Is my old lady tired? The hell she is: she's tough, she's brave, she's aware of life and she would take a congeries of eels over a hassle of bishops any day" (SL, 231). This decision to create a dramatic persona is a continuation of his need, first explored in *The Lost Son*, to create a mask through which he could work out his spiritual autobiography.

The protagonist of "Meditations of an Old Woman," Roethke says, "modelled, in part, after my own mother, now dead, whose favorite reading was the Bible, Jane Austen, and Dostoyevsky—in other words, a gentle, highly articulate old lady believing in the glories of the world, yet fully conscious of its evils" (PC, 58). The sequence was no doubt partially inspired by the death of his mother in 1954, but in addition her death and his own growing physical frailty must have provided an occasion for the shift in feeling and self-awareness that would give rise not only to this sequence, but to the entire range of poems in his final book, *The Far Field*.

"Meditations of an Old Woman" is an attempt to face—from a distance—aging, mortality, and various eschatological questions. By "distance," I mean that Roethke intends his identity to be subsumed by the consciousness of the old woman: she is *old* and a *woman*. Because we are asked to believe that the poem is happening in her mind, the consciousness here is more disparate, more radically independent from the poet than the lost son was or the aging man in "North American Sequence" will be. Indeed, the distance between Roethke and his invented old woman is, too often, not convincing enough, and the mask wears thin at many points in the sequence. Sometimes the old woman persona sounds too much like the lost son, too much like the naked Roethke of *Praise to the End!* or the aging Roethke in "North American Sequence." And at times she seems somewhat stereotyped and clichéd, her psychology not altogether convincing. Notwithstanding these flaws, the sequence is important because these poems show Roethke in the process of claiming a new form, a longer free verse line of often six or seven stresses. In this sense, the sequence marks a shift away from the metaphysical conventions of the love poems that had preoccupied him over the preceding three years, and a move toward the grand open form of "North American Sequence."

Regardless of the cracks in the old woman mask there is extraordinary writing in the sequence. Roethke combines a risky meta-physical speech with close observation and rich natural imagery. When he is most successful, the old woman seems to me to speak for the poet's feminine self. One might say that she stands for the woman in Roethke, or the idea of the feminine which he felt defined a part of himself.

"First Meditation" opens the sequence in the old woman's aging present. Her concerns are of the spirit, of the conflict between body and soul. Unlike the lovers in the "Love Poems," who found their bodies a vehicle to spirit, the old lady here feels only a painful dualism between body and soul. "The spirit moves, but not always upward," and "the rind, often, hates the life within," she cries. When she asks with an Old Testament echo, "How can I rest in the days of my slowness?," this becomes, in a sense, the representative question of the sequence. For to achieve an "old crone's knowing" will become her goal, and like the crones of "Frau Bauman, Frau Schmidt, and Frau Schwartze," she too must tap into certain cosmic currents and organic principles in order to know.

The first two sections of "First Meditation" reveal the old woman as a quintessential Roethkean character. Her fundamental place in the world is in nature and her primary concept of movement is the familiar Roethkean idea of the journey. Her sense of oscillation is similar to the lost son's; she knows the journey is perpetual and that the supposed movement is not always forward. "All journeys, I think, are the same," she says; for a while the "movement is for-ward, after a few wavers," but as the air of passing trucks blasts the "frosted windows" she goes "backward, / Backward in time."

Riding the night bus she brings to mind the young Roethke in "Night Journey." However, the movement into memory is accom-plished by Roethke's new longer line. And where else does the woman find herself in her reverie but in the greenhouse? This is not a lapse in imagination for Roethke, in that he claimed to have based his old woman on his mother whose life, like his own, was centered in the glass house.

Two song sparrows, one within a greenhouse,
Shuttling its throat while perched on a wind-vent,

And another, outside, in the bright day,
With a wind from the west and the trees all in motion.
One sang, then the other,
The songs tumbling over and under the glass,
And the men beneath them wheeling in dirt to the cement benches,
The laden wheelbarrows creaking and swaying,
And the up-spring of the plank when a foot left the runway.

Her memory gives her this comforting song of innocence. Yet as she springs to the present her journey is fraught with false starts and detours: "The ticket mislaid or lost, the gate / Inaccessible, the boat always pulling out."

From her meditation on the idea of her journey, she moves in section 3 into imagining the vicissitudes of her spirit's struggle. She likens her spirit to a crab "Grotesque, awkward," with "the tail and smaller legs slipping and sliding slowly backward," "Or a salmon" nudging "into a back-eddy, a sandy inlet, / Bumping against sticks and bottom-stones." Whereas this kind of identification with crustaceans and fish will come to define the protagonist's soul in "North American Sequence," here as these lines break open, ten or more feet, Roethke speaks loudly above the old woman's voice. The sea gazer and muck prober, he overpowers the "bird-furtive" bus rider of the first two sections.

Now, having merged her inner struggle to the natural world, like a Roethkean hero she is able to find something consoling in what she can hold in her aging imagination. Thus in the last section of the poem she calls that place where her imagination holds nature "the waste lonely places / Behind the eye." What lies there is a source of affirmative meaning that holds some possibility for transcendent experience—"The cerulean, high in the elm," "the far phoebe," "the whippoorwill, along the smoky ridges." These images open up, for her, into an oxymoronic vision of a flame not burning, and the poem culminates in a numinous moment.

A flame, intense, visible,
Plays over the dry pods,
Runs fitfully along the stubble,
Moves over the field,
Without burning.
  In such times, lacking a god,
  I am still happy.

The momentary fulfillment at the end of the poem affirms, if not a God in any orthodox sense, at least some animistic force in nature which allows her the possibility of self-transcendence.

As moments of stasis are always brief in Roethkean journeys, the next poem, "I'm Here," finds the old woman struggling with the joys of the sensory world in the face of mortality. The poem opens with the rhetorical question "Is it enough?" and this is followed by two stanzas of nostalgic images of the sensuous world: "The sun loosening the frost on December windows," "young voices, mixed with sleighbells." In her quirky defensiveness she says she is "tired of . . . / The April cheeping, the vireo's insistence." Only a bawdy humor keeps her honest, and as the stanza closes Roethke's play with Freudian images captures her fears and her charms.

> How needles and corners perplex me!
> Dare I shrink to a hag
> The worst surprise a corner could have,
> A witch who sleeps with her horse?
> Some fates are worse.

Her remembrance of adolescence in the second section is full of a young woman's sexuality—some of it sublimated in nature, some of it indicative of her own delicately erotic nature. She remembers herself as "queen of the vale," "Running through high grasses," her "thighs brushing against flower-crowns"; or she is "bracing" her "back against a sapling, / Making it quiver with . . . [her] body." As a young woman, she was in love with scents and smells and virile animals: "Fearful of high places, in love with horses; / In love with stuffs, silks." But in the indented stanza that follows she puts her past and present together and sees her adolescence and her old age both as transitional times of "intolerable waiting, / A longing for another place and time, / Another condition."

In the next section, Roethke reverses the stanzaic structure, and the indented stanza refers to the present. The dialectic between past and present is compelling here. Once nature was aphrodisiac-like as she caught her dress on a "rose-brier" and "The scent of the half-opened buds came up over me. / I thought I was going to smother." However, the meditations in the interior stanzas are a counterforce to the vitality of her lost adolescence. She dwells on the "evening" and the "ground-chill"—symbols of her aging self. The indefinable feeling she refers to is "A thing we feel at evening, and by doors, / Or when we stand at the edge of a thicket, / And the ground-chill comes closer to us." Feeling the passage of time in her bones, she imagines her body "delighting in thresholds," rocking "in and out of itself." The metaphor of rocking, which will become so important in "North American Sequence," here already indicates a sense of motion that unites the beginning and the end—physical birth and physical death; for Roethke it is a metaphor of the life cycle.

The poem becomes increasingly impressionistic as the old woman moves from a recollection of being sick as a girl to the present where her "geranium is dying," regardless of the care she gives it. Yet her romance with nature is characteristic of the dominance of the greenhouse world in all Roethke's major poems. Here the roses bring the old lady the kind of moment of "still joy" that the lost son achieved at the closing of "The Lost Son." The fusion of imagination with the particular meanings that Roethke's rose carries also looks forward to the epiphanous moment that closes "North American Sequence" in "The Rose," when Roethke exclaims, "What need for heaven, then, / With that man, and those roses?" In "I'm Here," the woman muses:

> But these roses: I can wear them by looking away.
> The eyes rejoice in the act of seeing and the fresh after-image;
> Without staring like a lout, or a moping adolescent;
> Without commotion.

Through the cumulative impact of nature, the old woman is brought to an aesthetic experience. She proclaims her faith in the continuousness of being, knowing hers is just a small part. Now her perception has some of the gymnastic dynamics of the lost son's, but she speaks in her voice, not his, an exclamatory voice more staid and meditative than the lost son's. Her imagery belongs to her female sensibility which can see its own shapes in the natural world. "I'm not far from a stream," she cries, and knowing that the stream is perpetual movement she believes "It's not my first dying" and feels herself entering into the cycle of birth and death that her new collective sense of identity allows her. The interpenetration she experiences between herself and nature—it is more than an embrace—is a nurturing, cosmic moment, transcendental in that it marries her to something wholly other. Roethke brings this to consummation in her final moment when the female and the male (wind spiritus) join. She is the valley—the vaginal cleft in the earth—as she summons the impregnating wind. The poem closes with the woman fully transformed and open to her vulnerability and strength: "If the wind means me, / I'm here! / Here."

In the next poem, "Her Becoming," the preparation of the spirit for some life beyond is the woman's sole concern. In trying to let go of the sensual world she enveloped in "I'm Here," she becomes a seeker of final answers.

> Soft, soft, the snow's not falling. What's a seed?
> A face floats in the ferns. Do maimed gods walk?
>
> ·
>
> A ghost from the soul's house?
> I'm where I always was.
> The lily broods. Who knows
> The way out of a rose?
>
> · · · · · · · · · · · · · ·
>
> Where was I going. Where?
> What was I running from?
> To these I cried my life—
> The loved fox, and the wren.
>
> · · · · · · · · · · · · · · · · · ·
>
> Did my will die? Did I?
> I said farewell to sighs,
> Once to the toad,
> Once to the frog,
> And once to my flowing thighs.

I excerpt these passages in full to illustrate how, notwithstanding Roethke's intentions, the old woman's voice not only echoes the oracular cries of the lost son but imitates them. The imagery, the four- and five-beat lines, the rhetoric of innocence all belong to the boy-hero of the earlier poems. At other moments the old woman sounds too literary, more like the aging poet in "North American Sequence" who speculates on aesthetics: "The moon, a pure Islamic shape, looked down. / The light air slowed: It was not night or day. / All natural shapes became symbolical." (The last line obviously looks forward to "In a Dark Time.")

For the most part, the poem is dominated by a kind of tight lyric intensity that the other poems in the sequence do not have. The poem opens, as the others do, with a narrativelike statement and quotidian details, but it shifts quickly into a language that is aphoristic and at times gnomic. The poetry is compelling, but it seems to belong less to the old lady than to the lost son. The nursery rant speech of the "lost son" sequence has returned, and though the imagery is somewhat different, the tone, diction, and most importantly the strategies are the same. This could be the lost son speaking in "Bring the Day," "Give Way, Ye Gates," or "Sensibility! O La!"

The old woman's bursts are crises of love and faith in the face of oncoming death. They remain the voice of the deep, irrational self that sees deepest in pure song and metaphor. In section 3 her cries become ecstatic: "I have seen! I have seen!— / The line! The holy line! / A small place all in flame." As the section closes, she is "rapt," as she says, both enraptured in the spirit and wrapped up by love: "I love because I am / A rapt thing with a name." The lovely embedded rhyme between "I am," and "name" amplifies and fuses the affirmation of being she feels and the source of transcendence that is in love.

Section 4 is one of the most authentic moments of the old woman's monologue. The *a b c a c c f c d d* rhyme scheme and the regularity of the pentameter give an ease and intensity to this moment of self-understanding. As she desires to be all atmosphere, she moves out of shape and form toward the air. "I hum in pure vibration, like a saw," or "By swoops of bird, by leaps of fish, I live," she says. A new kind of becoming infuses her as nature becomes one element: "A light wind rises: I become the wind." In retrospect, this act of becoming the wind seems to be an early version of a metaphor and an idea that Roethke would execute with greater effectiveness in one of his final poems, "In a Dark Time," where he ends crying "one is One, free in the tearing wind." As is often true in these poems, lines, tropes, and phrases will reappear in *The Far Field* with greater force and command.

The meditation which follows, "Fourth Meditation," contains some of the most and some of the least successful language in the sequence. Roethke's effort to get inside a woman's consciousness is more direct and in a sense obvious in a somewhat detracting way in this poem. It opens with the old lady meditating on her need for "eternal purpose," and her accreting imagination allows us to situate her soul in a complex but familiar landscape. As in section 3 of "First Meditation," where her spirit's sinuous journey was likened to the movement of a crab and then a salmon, here she refers to herself in an eternal moment.

> As a chip or shell, floating lazily with a slow current,
> A drop of the night rain still in me,
> A bit of water caught in a wrinkled crevice,
> A pool riding and shining with the river,
> Dipping up and down in the ripples,
> Tilting back the sunlight.

In section 2 her meditation on death and her spirit gives way to a speculation on womanhood.

> What is it to be a woman?
> To be contained, to be a vessel?
> To prefer a window to a door?
> A pool to a river?
> To become lost in a love,
> Yet remain only half aware of the intransient glory?
> To be a mouth, a meal of meat?
> To gaze at a face with the fixed eyes of a spaniel?

Roethke's idea of womanhood as vessel, opening, and submissive lover falls into cliché. Even if this kind of view is a social by-product of its age (the poems were written in the mid-1950s), and in all fairness to Roethke we must say that it is, such stereotypical perceptions remain unconvincing and one dimensional; in short they do not enlarge the psychology of his art. Similarly, the old woman's ruminations on the vain, gossipy, and materialistic nature of a certain kind of woman sound more like Roethke's editorializing than an old woman's high-minded idealism.

> I think of the self-involved:
> The ritualists of the mirror, the lonely drinkers,
> The minions of benzedrine and paraldehyde,
> And those who submerge themselves deliberately in trivia,
> . . . .

> Match-makers, arrangers of picnics—
> What do their lives mean,
> And the lives of their children?—

However, the second half of the poem breaks free of cliché as the woman finds her way into fresh and idiosyncratic perception. In issuing a wish for the led-astray women, she sees them in her most refined imagination as women of possibility connected to their origins in all creation. At such a moment Roethke's best writing dovetails with what is truest in the woman's imagination, and the depth of her personality emerges. She sees them first as "figures walking in a greeny garden, / . . . beautiful still-to-be-born," and then as "The descendants of the playful tree-shrew that survived the archaic killers, / The fang and the claw, the club and the knout, the irrational edict."

The poem closes with some of the old woman's finest meditative language. She finds a relationship with nature that is reciprocal and fused, and now her language holds at once her deep perception and her feeling. She can say, "This lake breathes like a rose," "I drink my tears in a place where all light comes," "Who else sweats light from a stone?" She possesses some of the self-actualizing powers of the lost son, but Roethke's language here allows her to break into a syntax and diction that belong to her nature. Her tone slows and a high rhetoric gives her closing confessions a credibility and dignity that are her own.

> Is my body speaking? I breathe what I am:
> The first and last of all things.
> Near the graves of the great dead,
> Even the stones speak.

These lines are the prologue to the final poem, "What Can I Tell My Bones?" In this crescendoing poem, the old woman's drive to apprehend the infinite is better realized in an intellectual sense and the language suits her purpose. The balance between metaphysical speculation, oracular statement, and concrete imagery creates a tension and originality that the other poems lack. Like the lost son and the final man in "North American Sequence," the old lady proclaims herself a ceaseless voyager—a "perpetual beginner" as she puts it.

The poem is structured by indented stanzas that contain her interior lyric cries. Her outburst in the first indentation, "Before the moon draws back, / Dare I blaze like a tree?," establishes the religious tone of the poem. In the stanza that follows, the natural world becomes imbued with a sacramentalism absent from the earlier poems in the sequence. She smells and hears in "a world always late afternoon," "the circular smells of a slow wind," or "the weeds' vesperal whine." The circular motion and the vesperal whine give the landscape some eternal resonance that will enable her to define her soul's situation.

The allusion in the next stanza to Whitman's solitary thrush in "When Lilacs Last in the Dooryard Bloom'd" furthers her sense of courage mixed with vulnerability. Given the imminence of her death—her "bones"—this bird singing "out in solitariness / A thin harsh song" is a singer of "Death's outlet song of life," as Whitman termed his thrush. In her ensuing proclamation—"How close we are to the sad animals! / I need a pool; I need a puddle's calm"—the old woman believes that those creatures can bring her harmony and peace.

As the poem develops into a dialogue with the self, she turns to the part of herself that encompasses her predicament as earthbound woman seeking the knowledge of God. In addressing her bones she confronts her most primary physical self—her mortal skeleton. However, each time she faces "the darkening shore," she sees in nature sacramental emblems ("The songs from a spiral tree," "Fury of wind, and no apparent wind") that pull her toward the motions of another self and give her the courage to confess her deepest fears.

The imagery at the section's closing alludes to Eliot, and the "man chasing a cat, / With a broken umbrella" is perhaps even a portrait of Eliot. So when the old woman confesses in the beginning of the next section that "It is difficult to say all things are well, / When the worst is about to arrive," the evocations of sections III and V of "Little Gidding" seem clear. The woman's spiritual desire has something in common with Eliot's at the close of the Quartets, but her way is less traditionally religious, and this must account for part of the meaning in Roethke's ironic inversion of Eliot's phrase. The woman's movement is backward and inward. She gains spiritual sustenance as she remembers her phylogenetic origins: "When I was a lark, I sang; / When I was a worm, I devoured." She moves continually inward and conceives of her being in its tripartite state—ego, heart, and spirit accordingly: "The self says, I am; / The heart says, I am less; / The spirit says, you are nothing." Having expressed her need for spiritual nothingness, she asks her marrow self, "What Can I Tell My Bones?," and answers only in oracular statements.

The remainder of the section is dominated by this sphinxlike voice so that her rhetorical questions pose her soul's dilemma: "Do these bones live? Can I live with these bones? / Mother, mother of us all, tell me where I am! / O to be delivered from the rational into the realm of pure song." Her questions and confessions have their own power now and are no longer reminiscent of the neurotic, compulsive bursts of the lost son. We can both hear Roethke and believe in the old woman when she cries out, "My face on fire, close to the points of a star, / A learned nimble girl." Finally, the religious point the old woman makes at the close of this section defines Roethke's peculiar disposition toward and in some sense his distance from the nineteenth-century Romantics. Her belief that "To try to become like God / Is far from becoming God" reminds us that for Roethke some pre-Romantic—what one might call a more orthodox—barrier still exists between the self and God. And though the old woman may be driven by the quest for perfection, she is not "part and parcel of God," to use Emerson's term. She remains a pilgrim energized by the possibility of divine knowledge.

The final section of the poem is imbued with a hylozoism that allows us to feel the union between the old woman and the world. Released from the "dreary dance of opposites," her entire way of feeling and seeing is connected with the most subtle aspects of the organic world and she hears the "barest speech of light among the stones." The elements are her direction now; "The wind rocks with my wish; the rain shields me," and light becomes her guide. "The sun! The sun! And all we can become!" may sound clichéd, but it is rescued and confirmed by the marvelous proclamations that follow.

> In the long fields, I leave my father's eye;
> And shake the secrets from my deepest bones;
> My spirit rises with the rising wind;
> I'm thick with leaves and tender as a dove,
> I take the liberties a short life permits—
> I seek my own meekness.

As the poem and the sequence close, the old woman becomes the Roethkean hero as empathizer. She recovers her "tenderness by long looking" so she can "love everything alive." When she tells us she is "wet with another life," she is not the lost son born to a world of cuttings, but an old woman born into a mature and sacramental self. Her biblical cry, "Yea, I have gone and stayed," puts forth a paradox that defines her reconciliation between the eternal and the temporal. Indeed, this cry suggests that she has left time through her epiphanous moments but has not left the ultimate reality of her bones. The spirit that makes things clear to her as the poem closes is "outside" her, is absolute and beyond human will. She has given up selfhood and she leaves us on a note of self-effacement and humility, much closer to an orthodox idea of God than to a Romantic one.

> What came to me vaguely is now clear,
> As if released by a spirit,
> Or agency outside me.
> Unprayed-for,
> And final.

As a whole, the sequence seems to me flawed, but a fully realized poem like "What Can I Tell My Bones?" reveals Roethke's ability to make the monologue work while still being true to his deepest obsessions. In retrospect, the sequence is, I think, a transitional group of poems pointing the way to the great final cycle, "North American Sequence." The move to the longer line, the meditative stance of the persona, the vacillation between the sweeping delicacy of nature imagery and the elevated metaphysical language, and the concerns with final matters are all more finely assimilated in the voice of the aging man of "North American Sequence." Many phrases, metaphors, and strategies in the "Meditations of an Old Woman" reappear in "North American Sequence" with greater conviction and control. The sense of wasteland in "First Meditation" is much more fully developed in "The Longing," which opens with a landscape that unites spiritual aridity with the physical desolation of a prairie landscape. The old woman's silent, solitary musing on "sandy beaches" in "Fourth Meditation" is far better developed in the aging man's gazing at the river in "Meditation at Oyster River." Or, the idea of being a "perpetual beginner," which opens "What Can I Tell My Bones?," is developed into a complex metaphor in the first section of "Journey to the Interior," where the poet dreams of "journeys repeatedly," of "flying like a bat into a narrowing tunnel" and driving his jeep "out a long peninsula." One could go on making these comparisons, but that is in the end unfair to the "Old Woman" poems. They are more important than just transitional poems would be, for they show Roethke revitalizing himself after the metrically formal love poems and taking chances with language, point of view, and the large hard questions from which he never shied.

SEVEN

The Final Man and the Far Field:
"North American Sequence"

As with the greenhouse poems, the "Love Poems," and *Praise to the End!*, "North American Sequence" assumes a whole shape; it presents a phase of being, an unfolding journey. If we look at the body of Roethke's work as having a continuous contour, then certainly "North American Sequence" is part of its form. Appropriately, these are the poems of "the final man," "In robes of green, in garments of adieu" as Roethke refers to himself in "The Far Field." Just as the urging, sprouting, and writhing in birth slime inform the lost son's experience in the greenhouse, and the seeing and suffering "In another being at last" characterize Roethke's journey into love in *Words for the Wind*, so his preoccupation with death, final ends, and eternal matters defines his sequence set in the Pacific Northwest. In a notebook entry written during the last years of his life, Roethke refers to his musing on the sands of the Puget Sound as "an eternal death-watch, this gazing at the sea" (SF, 136).

As Allan Seager notes, Roethke seems to have had a sense of his own end during the last years, and there was about him "a strange air of preparation." His physical ailments grew worse in the late fifties (arthritis, bursitis, tendonitis, high blood pressure), and he wrote at a furious pace, publishing sixty-one poems between 1959 and 1963, as if he were racing the clock. In retrospect, these poems disclose Roethke's enormous sense of his own death. They "seem prophetic," Seager says; "they read like last poems."[1] Indeed, Roethke asserts in a notebook of the late fifties, "Who loved his life can love his death as well" (SF, 117).

1. Allan Seager, *The Glass House: The Life of Theodore Roethke* (New York, 1968), 251.

For a poet of Roethke's disposition, facing death meant facing God—wrestling with the soul's final problems and with the uncertain gestures of the self. His sense of himself as a "man longing for God" (SF, 143) takes on a new meaning in these poems. Over and over he makes notebook notations about the soul's destiny and the possibility of metempsychosis: "O the thin cries of the spirit, the tiny landscape of the migratory souls!" (SF, 141).

Keeping in mind that Roethke conceived of rhythm as "the entire movement, the flow, the recurrence of stress and unstress that is related to the rhythms of blood, the rhythms of nature" (PC, 78), one can feel the immensity of release in "North American Sequence." To understand the full meaning of the sequence, both formally and conceptually, it is important to understand the influence of Whitman. Eliot of the *Quartets*, of course, bears a relationship to these poems; Roethke undoubtedly felt the presence of Eliot more strongly than ever during the last ten years of his life, as indicated in the letter to Mills when he calls Eliot "Tiresome Tom" and refers to him as a fraudulent mystic (SL, 231).

Knowing well the extent of Eliot's achievement, Roethke wanted desperately to do something larger and more dramatic than the *Four Quartets*. In "Meditations of an Old Woman" and "North American Sequence," Roethke is often in dialogue with Eliot. And he not only realized the impact of both Eliot and Whitman on his last poems but also understood the subtle relationship between the two. In the same Mills letter he says:

> So what in the looser line may seem in the first old lady poem to be close to Eliot may actually be out of Whitman, who influenced Eliot plenty, technically (See S. Musgrove T. S. Eliot and Walt Whitman, U. of New Zealand Press—again not the whole truth, but a sensible book.)—and Eliot, as far as I know, has never acknowledged this—oh no, he's always chichi as hell: only Dante, the French, the Jacobeans, etc. . . .
>
> Oh Christ, let's before the eye of God, try to wipe away the bullshit about both Willie and Tiresome Tom & say this:
>
> In both instances, I was animated in considerable part by arrogance: I thought: I can take this god damned high style of W.B.Y. or this Whitmanesque meditative thing of T.S.E. and use it for other ends, use it well or better. (SL, 230–31)

In his notion of form, in his creation of the self as representative man and visionary explorer, and in his conception of America as a primal territory that is at once a realm of consciousness and a geographical space, Roethke repossesses much of the meaning of Whitman. Perhaps in the most original way since Williams, Roethke takes Whitman and makes him new again. The expansiveness of "North American Sequence" and the epic territory in the poems lead Roethke back to the free verse form he used so successfully in the greenhouse poems. A poet with Roethke's ear, dramatic sense, and meticulous notion of craft finds the lessons of Whitman a challenge.

> I never could understand the objection to "free" verse—it's only bad, i.e. slack, lax, sloppy free verse one objects to. For the net, in final terms, is stretched even tighter. Since the poet has neither stanza form nor rhyme to rely on, he has to be more cunning than ever, in manipulating, modulating his sounds, and keeping that forward propulsion, and making it all natural. Instead of end-rhyme, of course, he has internal rhyme, assonance, consonance. But he can't fall back on tradition as much as a formalist. It's the pause, the natural pause that matters, Lawrence said somewhere—said it better, of course. He has to depend more on his own ear. (SF, 246)

Roethke understands the form within the freedom of free verse. Perhaps no other American poet since Whitman has used the long line in a way that is as dramatic and yet organic, natural, and flowing; the long line of "North American Sequence" is almost never slack or prosy because Roethke is always energizing it. With his ingenious internal rhymes, his dramatic rhetoric which creates a movement from the natural to the metaphysical, he maintains "that forward propulsion."

If "North American Sequence" assumes a religious and psychological dimension without forsaking its total commitment to place, it is, in part, because of Roethke's handling of the catalog. "We need the catalogue in our time," he says, "we need the eye close on the object" (PC, 83). Roethke's "final man" assumes a noble Adamic task; in conceiving of himself as an Indian ("Old men should be explorers? / I'll be an Indian. / Ogalala? / Iroquois.)," he sets out to be a native namer, a reclaimer of territory, the perpetual explorer. Like Whitman, Roethke is able to build a sense of reality from an accreting imagination, which gathers in a seemingly spontaneous way the multifarious phenomena of the world. And Roethke's gathering, too, is at once an embracing of existence and an act of primary creation which lets the poet become a namer, to use Emerson's term, who can name things both "after their appearance" and "after their essence" and who participates "in the invention of nature." In these poems of the American Northwest, Roethke revitalizes this Emersonian notion of the American poet as namer and seer.

This idea of naming that Emerson called a "high sort of seeing" is a result of the poet "resigning himself to the divine *aura* which breathes through forms."[2] Such naming allows the essence of things to reveal itself. Roethke insists that we "Leave 'truths' to (our) elders, and take on the burden of observation" (SF, 257). More than ever, during this period of his life, he believed that "we have forgotten the importance of the list" (SF, 260), and in his later poem, "The Abyss," he summons the spirit of Whitman outright: "Be with me, Whitman, maker of catalogues."

Endemic to Roethke's Adamic enterprise of naming is the horizontal ordering of reality, that act of parataxis by which the poet creates a nonhierarchic vision of reality, a democratic presentation of the world. Although Roethke's paratactical relationship with the world is not as radical as Whitman's, because it fails to encompass the social and political realms of experience, there is in this sequence parity between all aspects of natural life and the human self anchored in its existential dilemmas. In this sense, Roethke's Adamic cataloging creates a nonhierarchic sense of reality. The self lives in the flux of creation that it illuminates by naming. Roethke's final man, like Whitman's singing self, cannot exist apart from the enumeration of phenomena which comprise simultaneously the world and the self.

In these poems Roethke revitalizes, once more, certain archetypal notions of the American frontier and incorporates them into a mythopoetic domain. The American myth of the frontier encompasses, as Henry Nash Smith, Leo Marx, and R. W. B. Lewis show, a

2. Ralph Waldo Emerson, *The Selected Writings*, ed. Brooks Atkinson (New York, 1950), 319, 331, 332.

web of emotions, desires, historical beliefs, and spiritual yearnings. In repossessing certain elements of this myth, Roethke becomes what he must become—a native explorer uncovering the backcountry where transformation, rebirth, and some uncorrupt relationship between the self and reality are possible. He converts the meaning of a frontier into a terrain of the soul's progress (which is not always forward).

Roethke's frontier is a literal one: the far Northwest corner of the United States. Place is important to the poet who is committed to a fluxional relationship between nature and the possibilities of the eternal. On Puget Sound where land and water meet, Roethke creates a spot where he can test the meaning of the "infinite capacities of the unaided human spirit."[3] Roethke is a visionary seeker who must also be a cataloging naturalist.

Although some of Roethke's earliest poems, like "In Praise of Prairie" and "Night Journey," suggest his larger sense of American space and topography, here his epic disposition informs the shape of the poetry. He heeds Whitman's plea for the poet to "incarnate" his country's "geographical and natural life,"[4] and Emerson's prophetic invocation that "America is a poem in our eyes; its ample geography dazzles the imagination, and it will not wait long for metres."[5] It might be said that Roethke's exploration of the Puget Sound region evokes the archetypal image and overtones of the belief in a northwest passage to India—the passage which holds the key to the real meaning of the new garden of the world which America has represented for centuries. Obviously, for Roethke a northwest passage has none of the possibilities of munificence or exotica that India represented to earlier generations of Americans. However, it resonates with the meaning of exploration and the almost ritualistic necessity of making passage—of voyaging toward something unknown. Roethke's territory is the topography of a journey out of the self; there is no passage to—only a passage ceaselessly unfolding. What Feidelson maintains is fundamental to Whitman's symbolistic imagination applies as well to Roethke: "The

3. R. W. B. Lewis, *The American Adam* (Chicago, 1955), 22.
4. Walt Whitman, *Leaves of Grass and Selected Prose*, ed. Scully Bradley (San Francisco, 1949), 454.
5. Emerson, *Selected Writings*, 338.

ego appears in the poems as a traveler and explorer, not as a static observer; its object is 'to know the universe itself as a road, as many roads, as roads for traveling souls.' "[6]

In many ways, Roethke's notion of the soul's journey through a wilderness is similar to what D. H. Lawrence says about Whitman's American open road: "She [the soul] is to go down the open road, as the road opens, into the unknown, keeping company with those whose souls draw them near to her, accomplishing nothing save the journey, and the works incident to the journey, in the long life-travel into the unknown, the soul in her subtle sympathies accomplishing herself by the way."[7] On this kind of voyage the self and the world embrace each other; the process of going is dynamic and vitalized by the self's creative faculties, which define the unfolding road because on such a voyage the self is indistinguishable from its experience. The seer and the seen are inseparable; consciousness and reality are brought into their fullest dimensions, for the very going forth validates the meaning of experience. "The road was part of me," Roethke says in "Journey to the Interior." Such voyaging involves an unfolding kind of seeing, an opening up of experience which allows the poet revelation. This is fundamental to Roethke's visionary way of seeing, and it carries a great sense of spontaneity. It is as if the poet were defining the unknown for the first time.

Roethke's Puget Sound is a final frontier, a place of confrontation where the purity of experience and the power of human sympathy are unimpeded by the secular burdens that characterize the first poem in the sequence, "The Longing." On this edge of place the poet finds the spiritual equivalence of the pristine wilderness—a primal territory where man can face his "own immensity" and the meaning of time, death, and the eternal. If in the greenhouse there was a blend of the natural and the artificial, in "North American Sequence" we are in a world of raw nature.

This sense of frontier subsumes the poet's conception of self; the final man is, in many ways, a pioneer. A solitary, rugged individual pitting himself "against oblivion" (SF, 135), this aging aboriginal is not unlike our nineteenth-century heroes Natty Bumppo, Huck

6. Charles Feidelson, *Symbolism and American Literature* (Chicago, 1953), 17.
7. D. H. Lawrence, *Studies in Classic American Literature* (New York, 1953), 186.

Finn, and Ahab. He resembles one of the "roughs" hazarding what Whitman calls "the irregular hollows" of "The Open Road." In "Journey to the Interior," Roethke takes the road with its "washed-out interrupted raw places" and drives alone in his jeep inland:

> Where the shale slides dangerously
> And the back wheels hang almost over the edge
> At the sudden veering, the moment of turning.
> Better to hug close, wary of rubble and falling stones.
> The arroyo cracking the road, the wind-bitten buttes, the canyons.

Even as a mystic, he conceives of himself as a backwoodsman: "And I look with a hunter's eye / Toward eternity" (SF, 128).

As namer and aboriginal explorer, Roethke's path into the wilderness brings him, as Lewis says of Whitman, "all the way back to a primitive Adamic condition, to the beginning of time."[8] The notion that "the new garden of the world, should result in a History that rises, in the end, to an inspired vision of America as paradise regained"[9] underscores the teliology in the sequence. For the rose is the embodiment of the Edenic world of the greenhouse and of the child's prelapsarian mind. It is also the Christian symbol of paradise—the final unity which Roethke seeks in the last poem, "The Rose." This symbol of paradise represents the poet's primary yearning to transcend, if not the linearity of history itself, an ontological version of such linearity—the temporal limitations of existence.

To come to the place of the "rose in the sea-wind" is not simply to find paradise and lift the burden of ontology from one's shoulder's. Roethke's North American territory is a space where time converges. Here the beginning of time, the temporal world, and the poet's notion of the end of time must be reckoned with. Time and space are, at one level, inseparable in these poems. The topography of place is not only a metaphor for a frontier, but also a terrain that measures consciousness itself. Roethke's Northwest assumes another archetypal American condition with regard to time and space. Lewis' discussion of boundlessness in American Romanticism (which helps us understand the strivings of Whitman, Emerson,

8. Lewis, *American Adam*, 42.
9. Leo Marx, *The Machine in the Garden* (New York, 1977), 89.

and Thoreau and the confrontations of Natty Bumppo, Huck Finn, Ahab, and Jay Gatsby) also serves as a point of departure in understanding the complex re-formation of frontiers and spatial meaning in Roethke's sequence. Lewis describes the American hero in space as one who takes "his start outside time, or on the very outer edges of it, so that his location is essentially in space alone," and then his habitat becomes "space as consciousness, as the unbounded, the area of total possibility. The Adamic hero is discovered . . . 'surrounded, detached in *measureless oceans* of space.' "[10]

Roethke is a postmodernist Romantic poet for whom the frontier is not forsaken but redefined. In the twentieth century, and most significantly in the post-World War II period when such assertions of boundlessness, communion, and transcendence are exceedingly difficult to affirm, the poet of Romantic inclinations finds himself in a dilemma. Roethke, perhaps more than any other poet of his generation, is able to face chaos, disorder, and darkness and return to identify with the things of creation and "proclaim once more a condition of joy" (PC, 40). In this sense, Roethke is a poet of the *via affirmativa* like his boundless forefather Whitman.

Yet unlike Whitman's open road, Roethke's passage to the Puget Sound is marked with more snags and detours, with "dangerous down-hill places," and with water running in more unseen ways "along the narrow furrows of the shore." Roethke's nature is at times similar to Frost's; the ways of passage that are seemingly affirmed turn out to afford less than the poet had expected, with a process of undercutting and inversion forcing the poet back into himself. Although Roethke affirms the necessity of a primal territory where man can confront the dimensions of his being, the parameters of such a frontier are convoluted and ambiguous; nature on the Puget Sound is at once expansive and infinitely yielding yet forbidding, demanding caution. In short, Roethke's relationship to nature in "North American Sequence" defines what I think can be called a postmodernist and post-Romantic situation.

Hugh Staples in his important essay "The Rose in the Sea-Wind," Malkoff, and other critics have charted patterns of imagery in the "Sequence" while overlooking something essential. Staples insists

10 Lewis, *American Adam*, 91.

on establishing an allegorical relationship between Roethke's use of
the elements and larger values. He maintains, "The associations of
earth for Roethke are largely pejorative: in one form or another these
geological images come to stand for origins. . . . water on the other
hand, has the opposite associations—goals . . . flux . . . and
life."[11] It is difficult to think of earth imagery in Roethke's poetry as
being pejorative; the fertility of the greenhouse and the world of
Praise to the End! are full of geological substance. To read into
Roethke's North American terrain a pattern of correspondence be-
tween nature and meaning is to overlook the complexity of spatial
meaning in the sequence and to miss the dimensions of Roethke's
post-Romantic struggle. On Roethke's frontier where land and
water meet, the boundaries are sinuous and fluxional.

It is important to keep in mind that the setting of the entire
journey is a land of junctures. Roethke constantly takes us to a place
where things converge, boundaries dissolve into each other, and
parameters shift. Indeed, this is one of the primary meanings of his
Puget Sound; its topography and metaphorical meaning merge and
create, in the fullest sense, a symbol. Everything on this estuary is
fluxional and merging, and the poet's being finds its identity, direc-
tion, and possibility for growth in this ever-altering confluence.
That is why Roethke says so poignantly in the opening lines of the
final poem, "The Rose": "There are those to whom place is unimpor-
tant, / But this place, where sea and fresh water meet, / Is impor-
tant—." On the terrain of an estuary, land and water interpenetrate,
fresh and salt water meet and enter into each other. It is a place of
change and exchange, a territory where everything surrenders to
everything else and where life undergoes perpetual transmutation.
The spatial cosmos of the sea is transformed into an inland force,
and in a gradual and convoluted way land gives way to the wide
measureless beyond of ocean.

In such a terrain, the poet has a perfect medium for discovering
the convergence of cosmic with particular, *terra firma* with the infi-
nite beyond. Metaphorically, such a world perpetually tests the
meaning of limits and the parameters of being. The soul learns to

11. Hugh Staples, "The Rose in the Sea-Wind: A Reading of Theodore Roethke's
'North American Sequence,'" *American Literature*, XXXVI (May, 1964), 195.

live interstitially, its movement following the way water and land
join. This is a topography where everything is on the verge of hap-
pening, and birth and death, danger and beauty, the illimitable and
the slough are all in motion with one another.

> And the spirit runs, intermittently,
> In and out of the small waves,
> Runs with the intrepid shorebirds—
> How graceful the small before danger!
> ("Meditation at Oyster River")

In "The Longing," which is a kind of overture to the sequence, the
opening landscape embodies an entire psychic condition. For the
poet's spirit this is a dry time.

> On things asleep, no balm:
> A kingdom of stinks and sighs,
> Fetor of cockroaches, dead fish, petroleum,
> Worse than castoreum of mink or weasels,

Appropriately, Roethke is inland at the edge of a city, where "The
slag-heaps fume" and nature is rank as a "kingdom of stinks." The
world is a slough of despond and a more authentic wasteland than
Eliot's because it is so rooted in a particular place. Roethke's sense of
self-depravity is the longing of a saint's and his feeling of wretched-
ness is a sense of spiritual failure. In terms of Christian mysticism,
the temporal elements of sensuality weigh the self down. Drunken
and lustful ("Agony of crucifixion on barstools. . . . / Lust fatigues
the soul."), the poet asks how he can "transcend this sensual emp-
tiness?"

In this time when "the spirit fails to move forward," Roethke calls
himself an "eyeless starer." Punning on "I-less," Roethke is both a
blind groper in the dark and without center or shape—less than I.
Roethke's final man is naked, free, and alone, but as the journey
commences, he is almost the inversion of the assertive and frenetic
Whitman who opens "Song of Myself" with celebration. Here,
Roethke is closer to the theistic mystic who embraces his de-
pravity—"A wretch needs his wretchedness"—and confesses the
deadliest of the seven sins: "O pride, thou art a plume upon whose
head?" Here Roethke's longing to move forward, to understand,

see, and finally transcend must begin (closer to, say, St. John of the Cross, than to Whitman) in nothingness: "Out of these nothings / All beginnings come."

The building rhythm and expansiveness of section 3 bring together Roethke's longing with his present sense of deprivation. The rhetoric of the conditional "I would" generates a terrific quality of inertia and anticipation. The act of cataloging and naming is a counterforce to this time of nothingness, which makes the poet's condition more poignant and painful; the imaginative projection of the possibility of union with the world creates the real sense of longing in the poem: "I would with the fish, the blackening salmon, and the mad lemmings." Likening himself to Jonah in the body of Leviathan, Roethke becomes a seeker in the dark, once again on a night-sea journey: "I have left the body of the whale, but the mouth of the night is still wide."

Facing the pilgrimage into his dry time, he returns to the inland deprivation that is his state of soul. "On the Bullhead, in the Dakotas," in "the country of few lakes," he smells mortality, "the dead buffalo," and accepts the uncertain journey ahead. Answering Eliot's assertion in "Burnt Norton" that old men should be explorers, Roethke adopts a persona that is closer to Whitman; his final man must be an aboriginal trailblazer, making a path through a raw wilderness. Identifying with the Iroquois rather than the Ogalala, Roethke seems to reject the bellicosity of the wild Sioux in favor of the more sedentary, cultivating Iroquois. For the greenhouse keeper's boy this would make sense.

Although the shift to water marks a sense of relief and perhaps some sort of progress in "Meditation at Oyster River," the very complexity of the shoreline topography and the unpredictable current force us to consider the real web of uncertainty Roethke confronts here. The poem builds to the moment that Roethke can say "Water's my will, and my way." At Oyster River, the poet faces his first fluxional juncture. Here, where a river opens into a bay and fresh and salt water merge, Roethke's perception is as intricate as the teeming complexity of the water's movement and alteration.

Over the low, barnacled, elephant-colored rocks,
Come the first tide-ripples, moving, almost without sound, toward me,

Running along the narrow furrows of the shore, the rows of dead clam
    shells;
Then a runnel behind me, creeping closer,
Alive with tiny striped fish, and young crabs climbing in and out of the
    water.

Hardly a passive observer, Roethke is a cautious man aware of the
deep correspondence between the self's yearning and the convolu-
tions of the journey forward. After "The Longing," the problem of
beginning is first to recognize the currents into which the self must
journey. As the movement of the water builds in a way that is
desired and somewhat feared ("At last one long undulant rip-
ple, / . . . Slapping lightly against a sunken log."), the poet dabbles
his toes in the "brackish foam" and "retire[s] to a rock higher up on
the cliff-side." Unable to move with water at this point and to enter
the fluid complexities which the spirit must ultimately join in order
to gain the motion of growth and becoming, Roethke opts for a
contemplative moment and watches the coming dark.

As understanding becomes more crucial to the form and move-
ment of the sequence, the opening of section 2 states a problem,
perhaps *the* problem for the final man. Facing death involves the
possibility of renewal. The reader moves from Roethke's imagining
the "self persist[ing] like a dying star," to his wish to be with the
animals that represent the possibility of the self's transmutation into
innocence and beauty. The fusion of sound and movement control
the brilliance of these expansive lines; the poet moves back to the
water in a way that reveals the power of his visionary seeing.

What is seen is wedded to the depths of the poet's interior. The
correspondence between the water of Puget Sound and the tortuous
journey of the spirit is penetrated because the poet's external con-
sciousness is inseparable from the movement of the external world.
The world (the water here) is embraced in its suchness and absorbed
by the psyche; the self is effaced before a given reality, and yet the
imagination transforms such a reality simultaneously. This is one of
the paradoxes and struggles of visionary poetry and one of the
inherent elements of emotional volatility involved in the visionary
experience.[12] First Roethke perceives:

12. See Hyatt H. Waggoner, *American Visionary Poetry* (Baton Rouge, 1982), Chap-
ter 1.

And with water: the waves coming forward, without cessation,
The waves, altered by sand-bars, beds of kelp, miscellaneous driftwood,
Topped by cross-winds, tugged at by sinuous undercurrents
The tide rustling in, sliding between the ridges of stone,
The tongues of water, creeping in, quietly.

There is no aesthetic distortion or exclusively imaginative viewing of this scene. Imagination, sensibility, and the world out there are forever entwined. Roethke's close and painstaking observation—his persistent seeing with accuracy—enables him to make the complex movements of water into a map of the self's journey. We are presented here with a topography of unknown danger and difficulty. Indeed, this baptismal web of confluence recalls the lost son's cry: "Bless me and the maze I'm in!"

What we have here is the dilemma that the transcendental poet faces in our age. Unlike Whitman in "Crossing Brooklyn Ferry," Roethke is not able to commence his vigil by seeing "the flood-tide face to face." Yet he insists on the consecration of the spirit and the possibility of self-transcendence within the maze of uncertainty and the possibility of failed vision. The hazards along the way and the possibilities of annihilation must be part of the poet's striving for transcendental experience. And it is this struggle which I believe defines the postmodernist dilemma of "North American Sequence."

In section 3 the meaning of Roethke's "first heaven of knowing" becomes part of the catharsis of memory. Memory becomes mythopoetic in its ability to bring past and present into a moment of convergence, as boyhood experience and present reality are united in the poet's remembrance of a frozen Michigan brook breaking into water. The whole movement of the poet's being is baptized in this water of remembrance, the self brought down off the rock of repose into the violence and beauty of nature's creative power. As the "midchannel begins cracking and heaving" the force of release becomes sexual and emotional, and the river assumes the great accumulating resource of the imagination. In this painful and primal birth and release into the long waters that will eventually lead the poet to "embrace the world," Roethke trembles into becoming like the "whole river" moving forward.

The lullaby of the final section, which recalls the eternal cradle of

"Out of the Cradle Endlessly Rocking," affirms what it means to merge with water; uncertain longing has become realized desire. Now to lose the self is not to be an I-less starer, but a man feeling the power of surrendering to the *Other*. To say that "Water's my will, and my way" necessitates knowing danger the way "the intrepid shorebirds" know the perils of the ocean. The poet knows that to move is to move "intermittently, / In and out of the small waves"— and to move nakedly, with the grace of nature. Illuminated by a new light (one is reminded of the "shining fauna" of Williams' "Burning the Christmas Greens"), Roethke is able to face the interior: "In the first of the moon, / All's a scattering, / A shining."

Now, bathed in a new light, the poet sets forth once more, this time as a pilgrim and a pioneer weathering the way that at once opens to the essential self and leads out of the self. The imagery adheres with a quotidian fidelity to place while simultaneously assuming a psychological and religious dimension; it is a landscape which is, at once, true to the ruggedness of the final man's journey into a frontier territory and a topography of the soul's pilgrimage. If for the lost son to go forward it was necessary to go backward, for the final man to leave the self to seek transcendence and to face death it is necessary to find the deepest center of the self.

As Roethke says, "the road was part of me." The act of passage and the poet's consciousness are inseparable—the shape of being and the contour of terrain inextricable. This journey in a jeep through a treacherous backcountry begins "the long journey out of the self." The setting of the journey shifts now to the rugged terrain of the Tetons. In this difficult country Roethke moves through danger; at the edge of death, darkness, and the rankness of the human self "There are many detours, washed-out interrupted raw places / Where the shale slides dangerously / And the back wheels hang almost over the edge." He speaks constantly of traveling the narrow road ("the narrow valley," "the path narrowing," "the narrow road") and recalls the fundamental fact that the road to salvation is a difficult one. In fact, his reiteration of the narrow path recalls the words of Jesus in St. Matthew: "Enter by the narrow gate; for the gate is wide and the way is easy, that leads to destruction, and those who enter by it are many. For the gate is narrow and the way is hard, that leads to life, and those who find it are few (6:13)."

To "drive in gravel, / Watching for dangerous down-hill places, where the wheels whined beyond eighty" is to test the limits of the self's endurance and the spirit's intrepid forging forward. On this kind of journey where everything is at stake, Roethke rises to the occasion, unafraid to take chances. As he breaks loose to the open road, he affirms the meaning of being at the edge of existence where possibility is greatest. Consequently, in section 2, the poet accumulates the indigenous elements of his country. Nature and culture are brought into the domain of the poet's identity. "The towns with their high pitted road-crowns and deep gutters, / Their wooden stores of silvery pine and weather-beaten red courthouses, . . . all flows past," because for the poet who seeks the narrow path and finds an open road, the quotidian world can be embraced and brought into a unified moment (much in the same way that Whitman does in "Crossing Brooklyn Ferry"). The world assumes a voice, and Roethke apprehends that "long moment" into which "time folds." On the "dusty detour" he has found the "shimmering road"—a narrow path where illumination is possible.

The water that Roethke sees in the final section becomes an apotheosis of vision. In this parched inland, the poet's vision of water is not that of an oasis, but a whole merging sense of his being with the *Other*. It is a paradoxical point where the self can apprehend the divine. The soul is at a "still-stand," not a standstill because it is absorbed into the "flower of all water." Roethke here echoes Eliot's "still point of the turning world . . . where past and future are gathered" ("Little Gidding"). To be at a "still-stand" is the inverse of standing still; at this center of self there is no "fixity," to use Eliot's term, but, paradoxically, a deep motion at what Roethke calls "the imperishable heart of form," where the poet can begin to apprehend the eternal. Water is no longer a pond of the unconscious or a primal place from which the poet emerges as quivering man, but it becomes the "glassy pool" in which the eternal is reflected and the world may assume radiance and beauty. As the self moves toward illumination, it is able to "attain a radiant consciousness of the 'otherness' of natural things."[13] "I have heard, in a drip of leaves, / A slight song," Roethke exclaims.

13. Evelyn Underhill, *Mysticism* (New York, 1955), 234.

The poem shifts as Roethke stands "at the stretch in the face of death" and gains passage beyond the self—to "roam elsewhere." The poet begins to move out, "Beyond my own echo, / Neither forward nor backward, / Unperplexed, in a place leading nowhere." Unlike Eliot, for whom this crossroad into the eternal present must open into a comprehensive understanding of reality, Roethke is able to find the "nowhere" of selfhood where the limits of the temporal vanish and personal identity is lost to the *Other*. He is able to participate, with full being, in the movement of the Creator's time. It is the "light within" (to echo the closing of "The Lost Son"), the intuitive center of self, which senses this awakening. Roethke likens himself to "a blind man" who, "lifting a curtain, knows it is morning." In this moment of metamorphosis, to breathe is to be with the ebb and flow of the world's breath. As "The spirit of wrath becomes the spirit of blessing, / And the dead begin from their dark to sing" in the poet's "sleep," Roethke is able to unify time and move closer to God, because the mortal past and the uncertain future are resurrected into a present and poetic moment in which even the dead sing.

An alteration of land and sea marks the tortuous movement of "The Long Waters." The poet's awakening in "Journey to the Interior" affirms the need to return, once again, to water. Here Roethke faces his own hubris; the need to have more than a sympathetic union with the shy beasts and warbling birds is an acknowledgment of man's desire for God: "Therefore I reject the world of the dog / . . . And I acknowledge my foolishness with God." Testing, in a sense, his negative capability, Roethke proclaims his "desire for the peaks, the black ravines, the rolling mists" which are symbolic of the totality of terrain which governs the sequence. His desire for all dimensions of the unknown enables him to embrace the sublimity of the Tetons, the dark canyons of the interiors, and the mysterious coastal haze.

Returning to the shore, Roethke comes to a sacred place; the "charred edge of the sea," and "the blackened ash" suggest a place of holy ash. Significantly, Roethke returns to the juncture "Where the fresh and salt waters meet." Once more we are situated in the complex topography of confluences, "A country of bays and inlets, and small streams flowing seaward." The psychic equivalence of such a world affirms the possibility of the poet's joining with the universal current.

Summoning "Mnetha, Mother of Har," Roethke calls forth the power of divinity in the face of his own mortality. Facing the eroding world around him ("the slow sinking of the island peninsula"), he approaches death less as Stevens' "mother of beauty" in "Sunday Morning," than as Whitman's, "strong deliveress" of "When Lilacs Last in the Dooryard Bloom'd." Roethke, as Whitman, allows death to be a means of self-liberation and self-transcendence. However, as a postmodern poet he is unable to praise death in the exultant way Whitman does.

His immersion in this sacred sea place enables him to join past, present, and future not only conceptually, as Eliot does in "Burnt Norton," but organically and psychologically. *"In time* when the trout and young salmon leap for the low-flying insects" (italics mine), Roethke claims the particulars of nature in the estuary, and the glittering waves trigger the mind back once more to the greenhouse—to his knowledge of flowers. The greenhouse continues to function mythically as the place where the temporal and the eternal come together. Underscoring the importance of this sacred juncture for past and present as well as salt and fresh water, Roethke is bathed by the tenuous currents and "the thin, feathery ripples breaking lightly against the irregular shoreline," which continue to define the fluxional place where the interior (geographically and psychically) opens into wide expanse of cosmos.

In the final section, the "desire" wakened by "the sea wind" is the light within. As his "body shimmers with a light flame," he experiences a transformation of self and has what might be called an intimation of immortality.

> I see in the advancing and retreating waters
> The shape that came from my sleep, weeping:
> The eternal one, the child, the swaying vine branch,
> The numinous ring around the opening flower,

The numinous flower prefigures the eternal rose in the final poem of the sequence, and a gradual release of selfhood marks the poet's surge toward circumference, toward the laving waters of the world. The water that bloomed in the mind in "Journey to the Interior" is now the bloom of ocean into which the self is released. The poet is beckoned out of the self by the child spirit of his being. Wedding himself with the ebb and flux of water's way (recalling "Meditation at Oyster River"), Roethke can lose and find himself and claim to "embrace the world" in a way that follows Whitman's *via affirmativa*. When Roethke says, "I lose and find myself in the long water; / I am gathered together once more; / I embrace the world," he affirms, like Whitman who effuses his "flesh in eddies" and bequeaths "himself to the dirt," that the most radical act of self-effacement opens the self to the most expansive way of being—to becoming part and parcel of the Absolute.

"The Far Field" reveals that the inner journey is more than compulsive meandering. Roethke's need to constantly get lost affirms St. John of the Cross's belief that one must get lost in order to be found. Roethke's penchant for getting lost and taking the narrow way is essential to his search for salvation. He must "dream of journeys *repeatedly*" (italics mine) because the very act of going is the way to some ultimate truth. As Roethke dreams of "flying like a bat deep into a narrowing tunnel, / Of driving alone, without luggage, out a long peninsula," the topography assumes once more a condition of soul. These repeated moments of losing the self in darkness are moments of humility which involve an acceptance of ignorance and deprivation. Roethke's arrival at such points allies him with the *via negativa* of the Christian mystics who find, to use St. John of the Cross's term, that "abandonment of the spirit in darkness" is the necessary act of self-abasement which precedes the true unitive life. Thus he learns "not to fear infinity" when he finds himself

> Ending at last in a hopeless sand-rut,
> Where the car stalls,
> Churning in a snowdrift
> Until the headlights darken.

He assumes a new form; the self and water become inseparable: "I feel a weightless change, a moving forward / As of water quickening before a narrowing channel."

Arriving at the "still, but not a deep center," Roethke evokes not only Eliot but Thoreau. He recalls the Thoreau of "Where I Lived and What I Lived For" fishing in time's stream, seeing the sandy bottom, and knowing that although the current slides away, eternity remains—and also Thoreau meditating at Walden Pond, looking into the water of the lake ("the earth's eye" he calls it) and measuring "the depth of his own nature."[14] As he stares at the river bottom Roethke sees the soul's "still-stand." Once again, in a place of transformation and unformed boundaries, "In a country half-land, half-water," Roethke is renewed, this time "renewed by death, thought of my death." In a sense, the inlets and peninsulas of the Sound are, to use Whitman's words, the topography of "death's outlet song of life."

In the final section, everything surges toward the sea. I do not see, as Sullivan and Blessing do, Roethke's "final man" in this section as a Stevens-like figure who echoes the "central man" of "Asides on the Oboe." The final man bears little resemblance to the "philosophers' man" of Stevens' poem who "Still by the seaside mutters milky lines / Concerning an immaculate imagery." Roethke's old man is not a "glass man, without external reference" in some rarefied "jasmine haunted forests." Rather, he is close to the gurglings of his own flesh and blood ("faced with his own immensity") and to humanity; he knows "All finite things reveal infinitude" because he knows the birth, suffering, decay, and death of natural things—he has felt the universality of their condition. He has lived in the forest of the world with Thoreau's sense of the sacred. Roethke's "pure serene of memory" is not the placid realm of Stevens' aesthetic serenity, but a state of grace emanating from a persistent and self-effacing listening to what Nathan Scott calls "the world's great choral fugue,"[15] and from a lifetime of affirming a sacramental relationship with the multitudinous presence of otherness in all creation. In this sense, the contrast between Roethke and Stevens is dramatic. In Stevens' poem we move through a world of fictive imagination—through the "jasmine" forests of his impersonal "diamond globe." In contrast, the final man's imagination is attached with integrity to experience; we move from the

14. Henry David Thoreau, *Walden and Civil Disobedience*, ed. Sherman Paul (Boston, 1960), 128.

15. Nathan Scott, *The Wild Prayer of Longing* (New Haven, Conn., 1971), 85.

"Odor of basswood on a mountain-slope, / A scent beloved of bees," into the "serene of memory in one man" which opens into the circumference of all being. Consequently, circumference can become for Roethke a mode of knowing the unity of creation.

Roethke comes to his circle ("this first of forms" as Emerson called it) in a way much different from Dickinson, who went "out upon circumference" to a place of pure silence. He departs, more as Whitman does, in a continuous flow with water circling the great circle of the world itself. Roethke's winding waters validate the Emersonian idea that there are no ends in nature, but only beginnings.[16] As the far field of death opens into a ripple "Winding around the waters of the world," the final man seems closest to Whitman in "As I Ebb'd with the Ocean of Life," who feels his fate in "the rim, the sediment that stands for all the water and all the land of the globe."

The central symbol of the rose unifies the experience of the final poem. Roethke draws on the literary and mystical meanings of the rose as well as on the meaning of flowers in his family saga. Thus, he invests the rose with a new significance—a meaning that brings the more traditional notion of the rose as a symbol of unity, perfection, and love into an immediate realm of the poet's life journey. Through the rose he is able to return to his father, the breeder of hybrid roses, and to the greenhouse.

"The Rose" opens with one final confirmation of the necessary degree to which "this place, where sea and fresh water meet, / Is important." In Roethke's mythology this place where, in psychological terms, the river of the self and the cosmos of the ocean join is the volatile juncture of transformation and possibility. The necessary commitment to place in the first section involves the act of knowing the finite in order to realize the infinite. Like a Thoreauvian naturalist, Roethke creates the rhythmic beauty of North America's indigenous creatures: "the twittering finches," "the wingbeat of the scoter," "the sleepy cries of the towhee." "The Rose," like "Crossing Brooklyn Ferry," is a poem of threshold travel. In both poems, Roethke and Whitman come to a physical juncture, where they can leave themselves to merge with the multitude of creation. Whitman sees "the glories strung like beads on my smallest sights and hear-

16. Emerson, *Selected Writings*, 279.

ings," and Roethke, attuned to the unitive rhythm in things, "sways outside himself." In a moment of ordaining vision, the final man asks:

> Was it here I wore a crown of birds for a moment
> While on a far point of the rocks
> The light heightened,
> And below, in a mist out of nowhere,
> The first rain gathered?

The flux and motion of the self journeying forward is set against the permanence of the eternal embodied by the rose. The poet assumes the rocking motion of a ship which draws his being out into the delicate movement of "The waves less than the ripples made by rising fish, / The lacelike wrinkles of the wake widening, thinning out." Against this temporal motion, the poet asserts the meaning of the rose: "But this rose, this rose in the sea-wind, / Stays, / Stays in its true place." The rose is at once struggling to be born "out of the white embrace of the morning-glory" and moving with the whole thrust of creation:

> Out of the briary hedge, the tangle of matted underbrush,
> Beyond the clover, the ragged hay,
> Beyond the sea pine, the oak, the wind-tipped madrona,
> Moving with the waves, the undulating driftwood,

The rose, finally, assumes one further dimension of the final man's experience; it brings together the motion of creation and the permanence of the Absolute into the comprehensive meaning of the poet's past—the dimensions of a lifetime. In a sense, the whole body of Roethke's work prepares us for this final return to the greenhouse. The rose embodies temporal and eternal experience.

The final man recalls not only the exhilaration of his father lifting him "high over the four-foot stems, the Mrs. Russells, and his own elaborate hybrids," but also how the roses beckoned him, "only a child, out of myself." The rose consolidates the poet's complex understanding of time. It emerges as a symbol of unity because of its archetypal significance (that is, as a symbol of perfection and divinity) and because it regenerates the meaning of Roethke's entire life; it is a natural fact of his past—a symbol of the greenhouse, the Eden on earth. The rose provides the continuity that unites the final man with his childhood self and with his father, thus creating an eternal present in which past, present, the possible or the future exist together and bring Roethke to an apotheosis: "What need for heaven, then, / With that man, and those roses?"

Section 3 confirms this eternal present within the province of the imagination. The mind is able to make a single life into a continuous rhythm that invests a distinct place with the meaning of the self. If the lost son could hear "what sings! / What Sings!," the final man knows "that single sound" in which "the mind remembers all."

Unlike Eliot's rose garden in "Burnt Norton," which has a quality of enclosure, serenity, and limitation (a quality more characteristic of the tamer British Romantic imagination than of the more expansive sense of nature that defines American Romantics from Cooper and Emerson down through Faulkner and Hemingway), Roethke comes in section 4 to a primal, raw world.

> I live with the rocks, their weeds,
> Their filmy fringes of green, their harsh
> Edges, their holes
> Cut by the sea-slime

This ledge of rocks is a sacramental place—the inevitable edge of the harsh world (the "wind-warped madronas" and "half-dead trees") to which the poet must come in order to leave himself.

Here the act of transcendence involves the ability to participate in pure being, "Beyond becoming and perishing," as well as rejoicing in the phylogenetic history of creation which has defined one element of Roethke's becoming throughout his life. He celebrates "being what I was": flower, reptile, bird, and mammal.

> And I rejoiced in being what I was:
> In the lilac change, the white reptilian calm,
> In the bird beyond the bough, the single one
> With all the air to greet him as he flies,
> The dolphin rising from the darkening waves;

And as the final man rejoices in the "rose in the sea-wind" which gathers "to itself sound and silence," he performs with purity and ease a communion with the sea wind and an act of being gathered into the rose—of maintaining himself and losing himself at once.

EIGHT

Evening Air: "Sequence, Sometimes Metaphysical"

The Far Field is a complex book—complex, perhaps, as a final collection by a poet like Roethke would have to be. Stylistically, it is Roethke's most eclectic volume. The four sections: "North American Sequence," "Love Poems," "Mixed Sequence," and "Sequence, Sometimes Metaphysical," create an overview of Roethke's various temperaments. In "North American Sequence" and "Mixed Sequence," Roethke handles the open form of free verse in a daring, expansive way. The "Love Poems," though less powerful and ambitious than the earlier love poems or "Meditations of an Old Woman," once again make use of formal poetic conventions, interior monologue, and a woman's persona. The poems move from the sensual to the metaphysical, as his love poems often do, but they have little of the summer fullness that characterizes the earlier love poetry, and they reveal his preoccupation with death. In "His Foreboding," he acknowledges what he cannot escape.

> Is she the all of light?
> I sniff the darkening air
> And listen to my own feet.
> A storm's increasing where
> The winds and waters meet.

Sensing the imminence of his death, Roethke wishes for his young wife (Beatrice was only thirty-six when he died),

> May you live out your life
> Without hate, without grief,
> And your hair ever blaze,
> In the sun, in the sun,

> When I am undone,
> When I am no one.
> ("Wish for a Young Wife")

Roethke's preoccupation with final matters, his "final drive to-
ward God," culminates in "Sequence, Sometimes Metaphysical."[1]
Of these final three sections, "Sequence" is the most unified, in
Roethke's characteristically obsessive way, because each poem gains
dimension and meaning from the poems that precede and follow it.
Roethke's return to a more formal poetry enables him to create, with
the line, a highly dramatic quality—a quality of intensity that at
once holds and releases the mystic's passion. Kunitz's observation
that "In a Dark Time" is marked by a style of "oracular abstraction"[2]
appropriately characterizes the entire sequence. Roethke notes that
in seeking some higher reality poetic language must become more
abstractly metaphysical: "The body of imagery, possibly, thins out
or purifies itself or the mind moves into a more abstract mode, closer
to wisdom, in talent of a high order" (SF, 250).

Roethke's need to purify his imagery in order to make a stab at
wisdom is indicative of the degree to which this final sequence is
devoted to a more singularly concentrated religious quest. Al-
though Roethke has been always concerned with the spirit's tran-
scendent aspirations, the religious dimensions of his experience
have most often been intertwined with the psychic, sexual, and
emotional phases of certain temporal experiences: discovering the
greenhouse, immersion in nature, human love, an old man's jour-
ney through unknown terrain in search of truths that remain to
some degree rooted in the natural world. However, in these poems
Roethke's persona assumes an affinity with the saint and the mystic.
When he is confined in an anonymous, white-walled chamber he
becomes monklike, and when he is wandering through the stony
paths of an arid wilderness he resembles an ascetic abasing himself
before God. Sensuous reality and the ebb and flow of the quotidian
world interest Roethke less now, and nothing stands between him
and his primary goal of apprehending the Absolute. "Perhaps the

1. Theodore Roethke, "On 'In a Dark Time,'" in Anthony Ostroff (ed.), *The Con-
temporary Poet as Artist and Critic* (Boston, 1964), 49.
2. Stanley Kunitz, "On 'In a Dark Time,'" *ibid.*, 41.

poet's path is closer to the mystic than we think" (SF, 250), he says in a late notebook entry. Seeking God involves the purest knowledge of one's individual being: "I'm aware that among the expert (unfrightened) trans-Atlantic literary theologians to approach God without benefit of clergy is a grievous lapse in taste, if not a mortal sin. But in crawling out of a swamp, or up what small rock-faces I try to essay, I don't need a system on my back" (SF, 244).

The dualistic aspects of Roethke's sensibility and religious orientation are more predominant here than before. In a Christian sense, one might say he thinks and feels in a more orthodox way in "Sequence, Sometimes Metaphysical." Recounting one of his mystical-like experiences, Roethke maintains that although he feels a "oneness," "I can't claim that the soul, my soul, was absorbed in God. No, God for me still remains someone to be confronted, to be dueled with" (PC, 26). The distinction between the self and the Absolute, the body and the soul constitute much of the poetic tension and human drama in these last poems. Here Roethke is closer to the tradition of Christian mysticism than he is to the visionary affirmation of Whitman; there is less importance placed on the divine which emanates from within the sensual, and tactile, and natural world and more of an attempt to wrestle with the Absolute in often metaphysical and meditative ways—relying on paradox, "oracular abstraction," to use Kunitz's phrase, and using the elements (fire, air, water) and dark and light in symbolic ways similar to those employed by the mystics in their writings.

The movement from "North American Sequence" is not abrupt. Poems like "His Foreboding," "The Manifestation," and "The Tranced" anticipate some of the concerns of "Sequence, Sometimes Metaphysical," but no poem is more crucial in its anticipation of Roethke's final search for God than "The Abyss." Although I am not convinced that the poem conforms in its five sections to the five-step mystic way as William Heyen has described in his essay "The Divine Abyss: Theodore Roethke's Mysticism," the poem does reveal Roethke's concern with certain elements of mystical experience. However, "The Abyss" is more accurately a transitional poem between the visionary seeing of "North American Sequence" and the more oracular abstractions and metaphysical apprehensions of "Sequence, Sometimes Metaphysical."

The poem seems less to follow a mystical program or theory than it reveals a more eclectic Roethke making use of his several sensibilities. Reminiscent of the mad nursery rants of *Praise to the End!*, "The Abyss" opens with riddles of hysteria:

> Is the stair here?
> Where's the stair?
> 'The stair's right there,
> But it goes nowhere.'
>
> And the abyss? the abyss?
> 'The abyss you can't miss:
> It's right where you are—
> A step down the stair.'

The stair no doubt has a meaning related to the "secret stair" of St. John of the Cross's poem, *"En Una Noche Escura,"* as Heyen points out, but most comprehensively it is the harrowing passage to God—the seeker's narrow path. The poet is at the edge between the last step and nothingness. Moral disorder, deprivation, and lassitude (characteristics of the soul's dark night, according to St. John of the Cross) mark this "Noon of failure." The abyss is a force that combines "contradictory things . . . intense communion and exceeding emptiness . . . a Divine Dark."[3] The triadic lines of the first section's last two stanzas create a sense of stagnancy and breakdown.

Section 2 discloses a psychic crisis in which the inner self is assaulted by the material world. No doubt Roethke is alluding to his manic phases which often preceded his episodes of nervous exhaustion. As Seager notes, "Ted . . . always felt rich when he was 'high' " and "started spending money like a drunken sailor—the favorite purchases in these states were wallets and typewriters."[4] It is not surprising that Roethke should call on Whitman—the spiritualizer of the material—to come to his aid: "Be with me, Whitman, maker of catalogues: / For the world invades me again, / And once more the tongues begin babbling." Mental breakdown is a dissolution of the self which brings the poet close to death. As death "Like a nurse . . . sat with [him] for weeks," he emerges as a man able to search the dark, "a mole winding through earth."

3. Evelyn Underhill, *Mysticism* (New York, 1955), 335.
4. Allan Seager, *The Glass House: The Life of Theodore Roethke* (New York, 1968), 189.

There is both psychological self-analysis and spiritual seeking in the next section; the intensity of heightened perception (the fact of the poet's vocation) brings Roethke to the abyss. He must go to the edge, "The slippery cold heights," and endure the "terrible violence of creation." Such creative violence brings Roethke to God and to the center of his passion to know. He alludes to God as the great Yahweh force ("A terrible violence of creation, / A flash into the burning heart of the abominable") that the poet must humble himself before.

Rather than setting a stage of mystical progression, as Heyen says, section 4 echoes much of the visionary seeing in and through nature that is characteristic of the North American poems. Once again Roethke recalls the greenhouse. Desiring the eternal, he seeks the "tendrils, their eyeless seeking, / The child's hand reaching into the coiled smilax." As "Knowing slows" and "not-knowing enters, silent, / Bearing being itself," he moves toward "the breaking down of the barrier between the surface-self and those deeper levels of personality where God is met and known."[5] Yet here Roethke is unable to move in the self-abnegating way of the mystic toward God. Speculating about the self's fate after life, he is drawn back into nature—still the deepest center of his universe: "By the salt waves I hear a river's undersong, / In a place of mottled clouds, a thin mist morning and evening." Moving toward the quiet stillness which enables the poet to enter into contemplation, Roethke embraces "this calm— . . . A luminous stillness."

The final section vacillates between the visionary's affirmative way and the oracularly abstract intuitions of the mystic. Echoing *Praise to the End!*, the intricate wonders of nature embody the poet's being: "I receive! I have been received! / I hear the flowers drinking in their light." No doubt alluding to the idea of the mystic's necessary "marriage vow . . . the irrevocable act by which permanent union is initiated,"[6] Roethke proclaims, "I am most immoderately married." In this poem, unlike the mystic, he is not married to God or to any kind of Absolute but to the idealist's recognition that "Being," where the self may find God, is a realm apart from doing. He concludes, "Being, not doing, is my first joy."

5. Underhill, *Mysticism*, 304.
6. *Ibid.*, 327.

As the poem which opens "Sequence, Sometimes Metaphysical," "In a Dark Time" is both an overture to the sequence, incorporating the major concerns of the poems, and the *tour de force* of the sequence. Of the poem Roethke says: "It is the first of a sequence, part of a hunt, a drive toward God."[7] According to Roethke, the poem derives from what was a mystical sort of experience: "This was a dictated poem, something given, scarcely mine at all. For about three days before its writing I felt disembodied, out of time; then the poem virtually wrote itself, on a day in summer, 1958."[8]

The poem commences *in medias res;* we are in the throes of a dark time where dramatic paradoxes open the way to the possibilities of metaphysical experience.

> In a dark time, the eye begins to see,
> I meet my shadow in the deepening shade;
> I hear my echo in the echoing wood—
> A lord of nature weeping to a tree.
> I live between the heron and the wren,
> Beasts of the hill and serpents of the den.

Roethke is the saint who must learn to see and, in essence, survive amidst darkness—fear, doubt, uncertainty. With courageous despair, he expands his negative capability and actively goes out to "meet" his "shadow in the deepening shade." He embraces the part of himself already disintegrated into the unknown; he faces the dissolution of the self's parameters which allows him to strip down to that essential part of being where true freedom can be attained. Regardless of the various symbolic meanings critics have ascribed to the "heron" and "wren," the crucial psychological fact remains that the poet is between these two creatures—in some painful in-between place where "A man goes far to find out what he is."

The drive toward God must necessarily be a kind of madness— not of course pejoratively aberrant in any social sense—but madness as the most intense and pure state of passion. In such a state, "madness" must be "nobility of soul / At odds with circumstance," because all temporal existence becomes a circumstantial reality which presents a barrier for one seeking the Absolute. In this re-

7. Roethke, "On 'In a Dark Time,'" in Ostroff (ed.), *Contemporary Poet,* 49.
8. *Ibid.*

gard, heat becomes a central metaphor in the poem ("The day's on fire!," "My shadow pinned against a sweating wall," "My soul, like some heat-maddened summer fly"). The metaphor of heat embodies the excited self at the point of delirium, suffering, desiring. This natural and supernatural fire is an ontological reality, and the "purity of pure despair" is the anguish of the self accepting a condition of being that has no place in time. We recall Roethke talking about himself as feeling "disembodied, out of time" before writing the poem.

With an image that echoes Prufrock's self-crucifixion, "pinned and wriggling on the wall," Roethke suffers the agony of self-insight as he witnesses his other self—his "shadow pinned against a sweating wall." A lost son once more, he wanders amidst a saint's wilderness of rocks, affirming his trial at the edge—where being and nonbeing become almost indistinguishable. As Kunitz says, "Only two eventualities remain conceivable: disaster or miracle."[9]

Having struggled to the edge, Roethke shifts the dramatic action. He breaks from cognition into imaginative catharsis, the self and the universe comprising "A steady storm of correspondences!" Nature is purged and transcended; the imagery is supernatural: "And in broad day the midnight come again!" The death of the self, that fact which Underhill calls the necessary "stripping off of the I, the Me . . . self-abandonment to the direction of a larger Will which— is an imperative condition of the attainment of the unitive life,"[10] is nothing less than cataclysmic for the poet. Hence, the imagery suggests a similar kind of supernatural reversal of day and night which evokes the kind of trauma that one might associate with the occurrences following the Crucifixion.

The oxymoronic "Dark, dark my light, and darker my desire" plunges Roethke into the abyss where dark must assume the guiding force of the light; the poet must incorporate nonbeing into being, for only then is unity possible. In one final outburst of feverish madness which anticipates the breaking down of the barrier between the self and the Other, Roethke feels his "soul, like some heat-maddened summer fly, / . . . buzzing at the sill." This body-

9. Kunitz, "On 'In a Dark Time,'" *ibid.*, 45.
10. Underhill, *Mysticism*, 425.

soul struggle, a drama of a more Christian orthodox nature than we have previously seen in Roethke, precedes the unbearable climax in which the poet cries out "Which I is *I?*" As he dissipates his fear, there is apotheosis ("I climb out of my fear"), a merging of identity with God ("The mind enters itself, and God the mind"), and a release of the self that constitutes freedom and integration at once: "And one is One, free in the tearing wind." Jacob Boehme's notion of the unitive moment sheds light on the closing of the poem: "At once the cosmos belongs to you, and you to it. You escape the heresy of separateness, are 'made one,' and merged in 'the greater life of the All.' Then a free spirit in a free world, the self moves upon its true orbit; undistanced by the largely self-imposed needs and demands of ordinary earthly existence."[11]

The sequential structure of the next poem, "In Evening Air," gives the movement from one intensified lyric moment to the next a sense of dramatic continuity. The twilight perception is characteristic of the lassitude and despair of mystical experience: as Underhill says, "Many seers and artists pay in this way, by agonizing periods of impotence and depression, for each violent outburst of creative energy."[12]

The poem opens in a Keatsian way, with the poet sensing death amidst the season of fullness: "A dark theme keeps me here, / Though summer blazes in the vireo's eye." The vulnerability of the self pitted against the unknown brings the poet to a moment of artistic self-awareness, as he realizes the value of his poetry in the face of mortality. "Waking's my care," he cries, "I'll make a broken music, or I'll die." The humility and longing in the second section create a sense of dire need. Roethke echoes—whether intentionally or not—Edward Taylor's spiritual plea in his most popular poem "Huswifery," "Make me, O Lord, thy Spinning Wheele compleat," and creates a sense of self-abasement and dire need: "Make me, O Lord, a last, a simple thing." In this time of spiritual deprivation, the poet lives on faith and recollection: "Once I transcended time: / A bud broke to a rose, / And I rose from a last diminishing."

Light and dark create a dramatic seeing in section 3; the foreboding storm brings life to its most tenuous point. With imagery that

11. Jacob Boehme, *Six Theosophic Points and Other Writings*, trans. John Rolleston Earle (Ann Arbor, Mich., 1958), 207.
12. Underhill, *Mysticism*, 383.

creates a tenebrous effect, the poet looks "down the far light" and beholds "the dark side of a tree." When he looks again, dark is no longer distant but is now his condition—"a dear proximity"— which he embraces. To survive, the poet must embrace his own death and the unfathomable universe. As things continue to be revealed with tenebrific intensity in the final section, we find ourselves in an austere, candle-lit room—a holy man's setting. Like a monk, the poet enters into contemplation, that act of "profound concentration . . . under which all things give to us the secret of their life."[13] If there is a secret revealed here, it is the power of the inexorable dark not only to bring an end to what we think of as reality, but to transform the meaning of what "we do." Thus the dark gives his broken music, his poetry, a new urgency. Knowing happens in stillness. As Roethke bids "stillness be still," he recalls the mystic's credo: "Be still, be still, and know."[14]

The next poem, "The Sequel," provides a moment of what might be thought of as comic relief from all this darkness. With characteristic self-parody, Roethke mocks his hubris, admits his "foolishness with God": "Was I too glib about eternal things, / An intimate of air and all its songs?" He affirms the nobility in this folly—the poet's need for the pure indivisible life: "O who can be / Both moth and flame?" With self-humor, he sees himself a clumsy, feeble man seeking Truth, "The weak moth blundering by."

"The Sequel" assumes the major tropes of many of the earlier love poems. The dance becomes a metaphor for the unitive motion which brings poet, nature, love, and cosmos together. The bird is, once again, the solitary singer uttering poetry's pure song. Yet in this later, sometimes metaphysical poem an impersonal spirit, a ghostlike "body dancing in the wind" appears. She becomes a muse, "A shape called up out of my natural mind," which, in the wind and in the mind, gives the poet the power to dance. The dance confirms the perpetual unity through which Roethke continues his romance with creation. Looking forward to the final poem in the sequence, "Once More, the Round," he declares:

> A partridge drummed; a minnow nudged its stone;
> We danced, we danced, under a dancing moon;

13. *Ibid.*, 240.
14. *Ibid.*, 38.

And on the coming of the outrageous dawn,
We danced together, we danced on and on.

Love becomes the wraith impregnating the imagination in "Morning's a motion in a happy mind." The awakening of the imagination is a sexual experience here, and in this metaphysical coitus the spirit's love transforms him and he comes to orgasm: "She left my body, lighter than a seed; / I gave her body full and grave farewell."

Having awakened him to new life, this spirit leaves him in solitude and in awe and wonder. In the final section, fire and water become appropriate metaphors for reality. In fact, the predominance of fire and water throughout the sequence reveals much about Roethke's mystic disposition. The world, for Roethke, in these poems, is flammable, and everything is capable of igniting and being transformed. What Underhill says of the mystics' use of the elements, especially fire, as having symbolic meaning, applies to Roethke: "By a deliberate appeal to the parallel of such great impersonal forces—to Fire and Heat, Light, Water, Air—the mystic writers seem able to bring out a perceived aspect of the Godhead, and of the transfigured soul's participation therein, which no merely personal language, taken alone, can touch. . . . Other contemplatives say that the deified soul is transformed by the inundations of the Uncreated Light: that it is like a brand blazing in the furnace, transformed to the likeness of fire."[15] For Roethke, the flame is not only the embodiment of the divine, but the intense illuminative power that allows the poet to confront the possibilities of being. When a "single tree turns into purest flame," Roethke sees all life (the tree his most dramatic symbol of natural and spiritual life in the sequence) as that "inundation of the Divine." Once again, the austerity of a single room—the monk's chamber—becomes his habitat. "Pacing a room, a room with dead-white walls," he purifies himself with "that slow fire" and denies desire, surrendering the self to a larger realm.

"The Motion" extends the idea that the rhythm of movement is essential to the spirit's progress. Although the poem echoes a meta-

15. *Ibid.*, 421.

physical notion of love characteristic of the earlier love poems, here the importance of the soul overwhelms the motion of the body; love involves the stretching of the spirit. Rather than measuring time "by how a body sways," as the body-soul fusion led the poet to assert in "I Knew a Woman," now the "many motions" of the soul direct the poet.

In this poem love is the way toward all union. We recall that Underhill sees love as the means and end for the mystic: "The self may be joined by love to the one eternal and ultimate Object of love."[16] "Love begets love," Roethke cries. And the poet's idea of an embracing motion contains the paradox that in becoming, one can reach the still center of being: "I dare embrace. By striding, I remain." The creative act of love becomes the transcendent force, the "faring-forth" that enables him to "reach beyond this death." Now, full of faith, he finds lost innocence and affirms the possibility of being. Playing with the linguistic symbolism of "O," he evokes the shape of original unity—the form of all origins.

In the final poems of the sequence, Roethke continues to take the winding path among the rocks. The basic Christian truth that "the way is hard that leads to life" informs the struggle in the poems. "Which is the way? I ask, and turn to go," he says in "The Decision," "As a man turns to face on-coming snow." Although the desire to unify the material and the immaterial, body and soul, sensual and metaphysical, is prevalent in the earlier poems, these final poems move toward a more traditional kind of Christian dualism: the death of the corporeal self is necessary for the spirit to be born in full. Invoking this Christian impulse, Roethke says in "Infirmity": "Sweet Christ, rejoice in my infirmity; / There's little left I care to call my own." Accepting the decay of the physical self, he can say, "I conform to my divinity / By dying inward, like an aging tree." The death of the body gives rise to the life of the spirit, and as the "meager flesh breaks down— / The soul delights in that extremity."

That freedom and eternity are born out of wrath and death is an assumption behind the meaning of darkness in the entire sequence. Again, I find that Jacob Boehme's insights illuminate Roethke's disposition: "Fierce wrathful death is thus a root of life . . . for out of

16. *Ibid.*, 71.

death is the free life born. Whatever can go out from death is re-
leased from death and the source of wrath that is now its kingdom of
joy. . . . And thus out of death life attains eternal freedom, where
there is no more any fear or terror."[17] It is this need to embrace the
wrath of death that leads Roethke to say: "Blessed the meek; they
shall inherit wrath; / I'm son and father of my only death." Such
acceptance of death enables him to find new life. "The deep eye"
that "sees the shimmer on the stone" is the still self ("A mind too
active is no mind at all") that apprehends something beyond the
finite. Hence, it is the still mind that hears creation's music in the still
world. Roethke (who was proud of his knowledge of birdcalls) de-
tects a vireo in the woods, which sings to him of the spirit's purity.

> Deep in the greens of summer sing the lives
> I've come to love. A vireo whets its bill.
> The great day balances upon the leaves;
> My ears still hear the bird when all is still;
> My soul is still my soul, and still the Son,
> And knowing this, I am not yet undone.

Again the pull is toward a more Christian emphasis on the soul, and
returning to the infirmity of the body the poet looks toward the
"pure spirit at the end."

In "The Marrow," as sensual desire dies and the yearning of the
spirit grows, Roethke assumes a more ascetic disposition. He seeks
a saint's way: "Brooding on God, I may become a man. / Pain wan-
ders through my bones like a lost fire; / What burns me now? Desire,
desire, desire." The bones of the agonized speak the spirit's anguish
to be with God. Roethke, once more in a time of trial, cries out with
outraged desperation: "Lord, hear me out, and hear me out this
day; / From me to Thee's a long and terrible way." Like a saint wan-
dering in a storm, Roethke, in slaying his will, seeks penitence.
Suffering for his ignorance as man and for his distance from God, he
bleeds sacrificially in the most infrangible part of his physical being:
"I bleed my bones, their marrow to bestow / Upon that God who
knows what I would know."

"I Waited" and "The Tree, the Bird" are poems of personal rein-

17. Boehme, *Six Theosophic Points*, 27.

tegration. After the agony of alienation in "The Marrow," Roethke rises from the dust—"I rose, a heavy bulk, above the field"—and begins to move as if he were walking for the first time, as if trying "to walk in hay." Like a child, Roethke sees the world afresh, illuminated, "charged with the grandeur of God".

> I saw all things through water, magnified,
> And shimmering. The sun burned through a haze,
> And I became all that I looked upon.
> I dazzled in the dazzle of a stone.

Still, the mortal life of man's dust must be faced and journeyed through. The presence of the divine symbolized by the shimmering world, and the shadow of death symbolized by darkness and a road of dust must always be the two polarities of experience through which the saint finds his winding path. "I moved like some heat-weary animal," Roethke says, "I went, not looking back. I was afraid." Wandering through this arid wilderness, Roethke creates a setting suggestive of the Holy Land. He is lost amidst stony walls, rocky gorges, and donkey paths. Forging ahead on faith alone, he comes to a precipice where he can see the sea and feel the breath or spirit of God. "All the winds came toward me," he exults, and "I was glad."

The continuing exultation brings Roethke in "The Tree, the Bird" to an ecstatic experience of reawakening after pain and suffering. Although the tone of the poem is not unlike that of the child's in "I Cry, Love! Love!," the meaning here is much different. This is not the naive consciousness of the budding self, but the joyful outcry of spiritual man, seeking his final phase after having undergone much suffering. The tree and the bird (two dominant images in the sequence) not only assume their significance as natural symbols (the bird has been symbolic of the muse and the pure voice of creation, and amidst Roethke's sacred landscape, the tree has been a kind of axis mundi) but are also Christian symbols. The tree, a common symbol of the cross, becomes the tree of atonement and suffering, the tree of life and resurrection. The bird, of course, is the holy dove, the spirit, the holy ghost.

The forbidding, stony landscape of "I Waited" is now alive with transcendent force.

> Uprose, uprose, the stony fields uprose,
> And every snail dipped toward me its pure horn.
> The sweet light met me as I walked toward
> A small voice calling from a drifting cloud.

All of creation exults with the poet who is now "At ease with joy, a self-enchanted man." As the "willow with its bird grew loud," Roethke hears a holy sound—the single sound of beauty in God's creation:

> I could not bear its song, that altering
> With every shift of air, those beating wings,
> The lonely buzz behind my midnight eyes;—
> How deep the mother-root of that still cry!

The deep "mother-root of that still cry" returns him to the stillest center of his being where he can feel a unity with himself.

As time is gathered into the eternal—the pure "motion of the rising day"—the "white sea widening on a farther shore" becomes a mystical vision, a vision of an expanding, paradisaical horizon. The "beating bird, extending wings" against the backdrop of white sea is Roethke's holy dove, the spirit. The image even echoes Hopkins' wonderful benedictory image in "God's Grandeur" of "the Holy Ghost over the bent / World brood[ing] with warm breast and . . . bright wings."

Yet never quite otherworldly enough to forego his continual trials as mortal man, he must "endure this last pure stretch of joy, / The dire dimension of a final thing." As a Christian eternity becomes something real and possible for Roethke, in the face of earth's final things he must continue to embrace his joyful belief in the continuance of the human spirit as well as of the holy spirit. The soul on the verge of death grows "back a new wing" and dances "at high noon" in the next poem, "The Restored." And in the final poem, "Once More, the Round," which is a benediction to the sequence, the circle—the symbol of the origin of time and the form of perfection and beauty—becomes the poet's primary mode of knowing. Proclaiming "once more a condition of joy," he adores the unity of creation; he is one with all that he has loved and all that has made him whole: "Bird," "Leaf," "Fish," "Snail," and the "Eye"—the poet's imagination seeing and creating. "For love, for Love's sake," the poet's purest driving force, he celebrates no resolution, no point of termination, but man's perpetual joining with everything and his ceaseless continuance of that unitive motion: "And everything comes to One, / As we dance on, dance on, dance on."

Index

87, 91, 120, 144; *The Lost Son and Other Poems*, 2, 3, 4, 6, 41, 97, 116; "Love Poems," 117, 129, 151; "The Marrow," 162, 163; "The Manifestation," 153; "Meditation at Oyster River," 127, 138–40, 146; "Meditations of an Old Woman," 115–27, 151; "Mixed Sequence," 151; "Moss Gathering," 56; "The Motion," 160; "My Dim-Wit Cousin," 16; "My Papa's Waltz," 62; "Night Crow," 6, 21, 80; "Night Journey," 15, 28–29, 117, 133; "No Bird," 16; "North American Sequence," x, 27, 28, 46, 116, 118, 120, 121, 127, 129, 151, 153; "Old Florist," 58; "O Lull Me, Lull Me," 82, 92; "Once More, the Round," 159, 164–65; "On the Road to Woodlawn," 24–25, 83; "Open House," 14, 17, 18–19; "Open Letter," 65; "The Other," 110; "O, Thou Opening, O," 65; "Pickle Belt," 62; *Praise to the End!*, 37, 65–74, 91–92, 97, 100, 106, 116, 129, 137, 154, 155; "The Prelude," 91; "The Premonition," 24, 25; "The Pure Fury," 111, 112; "The Reminder," 24–25; "The Renewal," 111, 113; "Reply to Censure," 19; "The Restored," 164; "Root Cellar," 33, 42, 51, 53–54; "The Rose," 120, 137, 148–50; "Sale," 16, 23; "Sensibility! Oh La!," 81, 82, 122; "The Sequel," 159; "Sequence, Sometimes Metaphysical," x, 13, 151–53; "The Shape of the Fire," 87, 90; "She," 110; "The Signals," 20, 21; "Silence," 21; "Slow Season," 15, 27–28; "Some Remarks on Rhythm," 69; "Some Self-Analysis," 26; *Straw for the Fire*, 31; "The Swan," 114; "The Tranced," 153; "The Tree, The Bird," 162–63; "The Unextinguished," 20, 21; "The Voice," 109; "The Waking," 12, 95; *The Waking*, 59; "Weed Puller," 33, 42, 53–56; "What Can I Tell My Bones?," 124–27; "Where Knock Is Open Wide," 74–76, 83, 91; "Words for

the Wind," 106; *Words for the Wind*, x, 96, 97, 115, 129
Roethke, William (grandfather), 26
Romanticism, 12–13, 27, 35, 109, 126, 150. *See also* American Transcendentalism

St. Francis of Assisi, 34
St. John of the Cross, 34, 112, 146, 154
St. Matthew, 142
St. Paul, 106
St. Theresa of Avila, 34
Schwartz, Delmore, 8, 37, 73, 111. *See also* Middle generation of poets
Seager, Allan, 34
Sexton, Anne: 2, 5; *The Lost Son*'s influence on, 3
Shapiro, Karl, 37. *See also* Middle generation of poets
Smart, Christopher: "Song to David," 74, 105
Smith, Henry Nash, 132
Snodgrass, W. D., 5
Staples, Hugh, 156
Stevens, Wallace: 2, 11; "Asides on the Oboe," 147; "The Idea of Order at Key West," 103; "Sunday Morning," 4, 145
Sutton, Walter, 36

Taylor, Edward, 158–59
Traherne, Thomas, 70
Thoreau, Henry David: 136; "Where I Lived and What I Lived For," 146–47

Underhill, Evelyn: 97, 157, 160; as influence on Roethke, 13; *Mysticism*, 13, 34

Valery, Paul, 73
Vaughan, Henry, 16, 69
Via affirmativa, 103
Visionary sensibility in Roethke's poems, 87, 89–90, 140–41, 153

Waggoner, Hyatt H., 2, 16, 89
Werner, William, 115
Whitman, Walt: 30, 72, 101, 109–10,

AUG 05

Printed in the United States
19762LVS00005B/329